How To Retire Early

*Your Guide to Getting Rich Slowly
and Retiring on Less*

BY ROBERT & ROBIN CHARLTON

How To Retire Early: Your Guide to Getting Rich Slowly and Retiring on Less
ISBN: 978-1482653724
First Edition

Author website: http://www.wherewebe.com

Table of Contents

Introduction

At the age of 28 my wife and I had just $16.88 to our name. I still have the checkbook showing that disheartening little entry next to the date of August 15, 1991. We owned no home. We were renters in an apartment in Boulder, Colorado and we were getting seriously worried because our monthly rent had just shot up and we had no clear way of paying it. I was unemployed and couldn't even find temp work. We had college and car loans to pay off. My wife Robin was working as a travel agent for the painfully low sum of $14,000 per year. She was frazzled enough about our financial situation that she was talking about taking on a second job at a local convenience store just to make ends meet.

At least she had a job. Since moving from Boston in January 1990, the best I had been able to manage was temp work as a word processor making $7 per hour. I had a string of failed career attempts behind me and no clear career path in sight. I was six years out of college and going nowhere fast. How had I managed to make so many wrong turns since college? Was I ever going to turn things around? Sometimes it seemed like the answer the universe was giving me was a resounding no.

Is Retiring Early Really Possible?

We begin our book at the financial low point of our lives to make it clear that even from unpromising beginnings such as these it is possible to get back on track and retire early. Not through get-rich-quick schemes but through simple hard work and consistent savings. No matter what your starting point, no matter how hopeless things may look right now, you can change your life around and set yourself on a path towards financial independence.

And it doesn't have to take forever. We did it in just 15 years, beginning in 1992 when we bought our first home and ending in 2006 when we walked away from our full-time jobs for the last time, hardly able to believe it ourselves. We were 43 years old at the time and had managed to scrimp and save our way to nearly a million dollars – enough to buy us a simple early retirement.

Frankly, if we can do it, so can you. This book is designed to show you how. It proposes a "get rich slow" approach to early retirement that has nothing to do with market timing, day trading, options, or high-risk investments of any kind. Rather, it provides practical advice on how to set a realistic retirement goal 15 or 20 years down the line and take the necessary steps to achieve it.

These steps are surprisingly simple. They don't require an advanced degree in business or finance. Just about anyone can do it, including you, as long as you take a self-disciplined, slow-and-steady approach to investing.

So let's get started by answering a few questions you may be wondering about.

Who Is This Book For?

This book is primarily aimed at hopeful early retirees in their twenties and thirties. However, anyone – including those in their forties or early fifties who are just getting started saving for retirement in a meaningful way – can use the concepts in this book to retire in 15 to 20 years. In fact, latecomers to the game may be able to retire in just 10 years. Why? Because they may already have a higher salary, more home equity, and more money set aside than younger investors, giving them a leg up. Empty nesters may also have fewer distractions, financial and otherwise, allowing them to focus in on their retirement goal with greater intensity.

If you already have a high-powered salary and are able to live very well in the present while also investing large sums of money for the future, then you probably don't need this book. In fact much of the advice it offers may sound strange to your ears. Why bother making sacrifices and getting rich slowly if you are already on the fast track to financial freedom?

But for the rest of us, it's good to know there is an alternative approach to achieving financial independence. It takes a slower track but gets you there all the same, and we think a slower track is much better than no track at all.

Why All the Specifics?

We intend to be as up-front and honest with you as possible in this book and not sugar-coat the truth. We lay our own finances bare, showing you how we got where we got and how long it took. We give you hard numbers on what we earned, how much we saved per year, and how much we spend per year now that we're retired. We'll share with you the simple Excel spreadsheet we set up to track our investments. We'll tell you where we went wrong and what we would have done differently if we had it to do over.

Of course the specifics of your own situation will differ from ours, but our feeling is that the more concrete, quantifiable information you have, the easier it will be for you to plan your own early retirement. You can extrapolate from the specifics we provide and apply that information to your own situation. If you happen to live in a very expensive city like New York City or San Francisco, for example, you may have to compensate for the much higher cost of living there by adjusting our income and expense information upwards.

Are You Financial Experts?

We aren't financial experts but we do consider ourselves financially savvy. I passed the Series 7 Exam and actually worked a brief stint as a licensed stockbroker early on in my career before deciding to take a different tack. But we both learned the most about investing simply by doing it over the past two decades: what works, what doesn't work, what's the simplest approach, and what may sound good on paper but isn't so good in practice. We made enough mistakes along the way to serve as human guinea pigs for what doesn't work, and we share those mistakes with you in this book so your own path can be a little easier.

Frankly, we think we have something interesting to say not because we're experts but because we're not. We're ordinary people who set a long-term financial goal and achieved it. If you're looking for specialized advice from a financial guru, we suggest you look elsewhere. But if you want practical guidance with plenty of examples on how to retire early from people who have been where you are now, you may want to consider what we have to say. We're probably not all that different from you, and it can help to get the perspective of other travelers who have ventured down the same road you're thinking of taking.

Did You Have High-Powered Jobs?

I worked primarily as a technical writer and proposal coordinator in the aerospace industry, and my wife worked as a travel agent then as a registered nurse. Our jobs started off paying poorly and got better with time, as most people's do, but neither would be considered high-powered. In fact our *combined* gross salaries for the 15 years from 1992 to 2006 averaged just over $89,000.

Most people take comfort in hearing we were able to achieve our early retirement dreams with relatively normal jobs. We provide our annual salary information and investment amounts in this book so you can judge for yourself.

Did You Get Any Financial Help?

We had no financial help in achieving our early retirement goals. We did not receive an inheritance. We did not win the lottery. There was no trust fund to draw from, no cash settlement, and no secret gifts of money from rich parents to see us through hard times. We have been financially independent throughout our adult lives, and we like it that way.

In the interests of full disclosure, our parents did pay for most of our college education (but not graduate school or nursing school), and they did loan us $7,000 to help with the downpayment on our first home back in 1991 – an amount we paid back over the next three years, with 8% interest. We mention this up front so you can decide for yourself if we achieved our early retirement goal essentially on our own.

Do You Have Children?

We don't have children, and that did of course make it easier for us to retire early. While we had originally planned on having kids, the universe had different ideas for us, so early retirement became our plan B. Given our modest salaries during most of our investing years, we can say with some certainty we would *not* have been able to retire at age 43 with children. However, we believe we still could have retired by age 50 or earlier with children.

If you have kids or plan on having them, you can still use the concepts in this book to retire early: you simply may want to give yourself some extra time to achieve your goal. Instead of a 15-year plan, you may want to put together a 20-year plan. That way, if you were to start investing by age 30, you could still retire before age 50. The power of compounding is such that an extra five or ten years of investing (and not drawing down on your investments) can make a huge difference, even if the amounts invested per year are smaller than they would have been otherwise due to the myriad expenses associated with children.

What's It Like Being Retired Early?

Early retirement is one of the few things in life that really lives up to its expectations. It's worth every penny you put into it. It's worth the years of sacrifice to achieve. And achieving it on your own will give you a sense of satisfaction and accomplishment in its own right.

While we don't want to bore you with endless tales of our adventures since retiring, we do want to inspire you with what's possible once your time is your own, so we'll briefly mention our very first trip after retiring and let that speak for all the rest. In 2007, celebrating our newfound freedom, we went on a five-month trip to New Zealand and Fiji and pushed our personal limits with adventures like skydiving, bungee jumping, hang gliding, jet boating, and aerobatic flying. We swam with dolphins and seals, snorkeled with sharks and manta rays, romped with lion cubs, rolled downhill in a Zorb, kayaked in Doubtful Sound, and logged 300 miles on New Zealand trails, including such Great Walks as the Milford, Routeburn, Kepler, and Abel Tasman tracks. In short, we had a blast, and so can you once you retire early. If you'd like to read more about these and other adventures we've had, you can check out our personal website at wherewebe.com.

We're at an interesting juncture in our own lives right now, having had 15 years of experience working towards early retirement and 6 years of experience being retired and seeing what it's like on the other side. (Spoiler alert: It's great!) That gives us some useful perspective on both sides of the great retirement divide. We hope we can answer a few questions you've wanted to ask but haven't been sure *who* to ask. And maybe we can even answer a question or two you haven't thought to ask yet.

If we can empower you to stop dreaming and start planning, to stop wishing and start willing your early retirement into existence, we'll have done what we set out to do in this book.

Chapter 1.
Getting Started

So you've decided early retirement sounds good to you. In fact you think it sounds great and would suit you to a tee. Traveling the world, rediscovering leisure time, turning happy hours into happy days (and weeks and months and years), following your dreams wherever they may lead....Yeah, sure, you could get used to that.

So you know *what* you want, you're just not sure how to get there. But you've started asking questions: What would it take to make it happen? How much would I need to save up? How many years would it take? How exactly would I get started?

Well, in a way you've already gotten started just by asking those questions. You're already on the move mentally and that's a good thing, because getting started is in many ways the hardest part.

Inertia makes it easy to keep doing the same old same old, especially when making a change means doing something hard, like going to the gym for the first time or changing your spending habits so you can begin saving for retirement. Putting such things off makes perfect sense, doesn't it? But you've got to take the plunge at some point, and that time may as well be now, since none of us is getting any younger.

The good news is, inertia works in two ways. It's true that an object at rest tends to stay at rest, but it's also true that an object in motion tends to stay in motion. If you can get yourself moving in the right direction, then the likelihood is you'll *keep* moving in that direction – and maybe even gain momentum through the years – right towards financial independence and early retirement.

Our goal is to get you moving in that direction. And the first step doesn't even require you to get up off the couch.

Declare Independence

The founding fathers declared independence before they actually achieved it, and so should you. They knew they had a hard fight ahead of them, but that didn't stop them from putting their intentions down on paper and declaring their liberty to the world. That was on July 4, 1776, seven years before the Revolutionary War actually ended in 1783.

So it's reasonable to ask, When did they actually become free? From a certain standpoint they became free the moment they declared themselves independent and saw themselves as free. Once *you* declare your financial independence and set your whole heart and soul on it, you've changed your mental outlook on life and your expectations for the future. At that point you've already won the first battle in your campaign for financial freedom.

In the early years of the war, General Washington marked Independence Day 1778 with an artillery salute and a double ration of rum for his soldiers. We recommend you do something similar to celebrate in the midst of your campaign. An artillery salute might be a bit extreme, but a double ration of rum or a fine bottle of wine might do the trick. While you're savoring it, remind yourself what you're fighting for: a life far removed from the rat race, liberty from the tyranny of stress and money worries, and of course the pursuit of happiness.

So pick a day. Maybe it's your birthday or your anniversary or the last day of the calendar year. Pick a date and put a circle around it. Now visualize retiring on that date 15 to 20 years from now – and celebrate each year as you move closer to your goal.

In our case we chose December 20, our wedding anniversary, as our financial independence day. We had extra reason to rejoice each year as December 20 rolled around. It may sound corny, but trust us, having a date to celebrate makes it all seem a bit more real – and you need that in the early years. It takes a lot of faith to believe that puny little account you just opened with a few hundred dollars in it can someday transform itself into the engine that will power your retirement, but it can, and it will.

Set Your Goal

This book will help you develop a detailed investment plan tailored to your own financial situation, but you can get started right now by setting a preliminary goal. We suggest setting it for something other than 40 or 50 years in the future. That's too distant. You really *might* want to retire in the old-fashioned sense of the word and simply lie down for a good long nap by that point. We think even 30 years from now is too far off. No, you need a goal that is attainable but not too remote. If it's too distant it will feel unreal, like a shimmering mirage that never gets any closer.

We think 15 to 20 years is ideal, with 25 years being the outer limit for a realistic early retirement goal you can still get excited about. That timeframe will give you plenty of time to achieve your goal without being so far removed it feels dreamlike.

You want your goal to have some solidity to it, some *heft*. You want to be able to pick it up in your hands and turn it around and say, "Yes, that's what I want. That's why I'm willing to work hard right now. And the sooner I get started, the sooner I'll get there."

Specifically, we would recommend:

- 15 years if you are highly ambitious, motivated, and have no kids (and don't plan on having them)

- 20 years if you have kids but are at least as ambitious and motivated as your double-income-no-kids (DINK) and single friends

- 25 years if you have kids and are reasonably motivated but also want to live a little more along the way

Now, these recommendations aren't set in stone. If you are super-earners or super-savers extraordinaire, you might be able to do even better than these goals. You might retire in just 10 years, say, if you have a high-paying job, save aggressively, and get a solid leg up from the markets. Or you may already have a little retirement money set aside, in which case you're already ahead of the game and may be able to retire a little sooner.

Nor is it impossible to have kids and retire in 15 years – especially if you have salaries that are well above average – but it's certainly more challenging. That's why, for sanity's sake if nothing else, we suggest you tack on a few extra years to give your investments (and your kids) more time to grow.

If you don't want to push so hard and aren't chomping at the bit to retire uncommonly early, you can set your goal for 25 or even 30 years down the road and allow yourself a bit more freedom to live in the present while also saving for the future. It's up to you: as long as you have a goal you can get excited about, that's the main thing.

One of the fundamental purposes of this book is to help you refine your preliminary goal to make sure it's achievable. How much you'll need to save each year, how big your nest egg needs to be, where to invest your money, how much you can expect the markets to return, how to track your actual progress against goals, and how to fine-tune your investment plan are all topics at the heart of this book. Starting in the very next chapter we'll provide you with plenty of concrete details and real-life examples from our own experience so you can see how a plan on paper can become a reality in life.

Work With a Purpose

"Right at this moment I hate my job so much I could spit. Sitting here at this desk for the next 30 years sounds like hell to me."

I wrote these words in a journal I kept very early on in my career when I was frankly miserable. I felt trapped in my job as a novice technical writer and I wanted out. It didn't help that the firm I was working for was being bought out by another company and a full tenth of the employees had been laid off. There was a malaise in the air that made it hard to be at work each day.

Unfortunately a lot of people feel a similar sense of despair at the drudgery of their jobs. Recent surveys have found that nearly 60% of Americans are not happy at their work and would choose a different career if they could over what they do now. Feeling trapped and frustrated, stressed out and unhappy, is the regrettable first stage many of us have to pass through before we form the hard resolve it takes to retire early.

If you find yourself in a similar situation, take heart: things do get better. Simply having a plan for early retirement can give you a renewed sense of hope. From the very start of our 15-year plan, I felt like I could see light at the end of the tunnel, no matter how dim. It made my job better just knowing I wasn't chained to it forever like a slave to the oars of a galley ship.

And once we started taking concrete steps towards achieving our goal – most importantly by making regular investments each month – it changed my attitude even more. I recommitted to work because now I realized I had a stake in earning a better salary. It was no longer just about paying the bills and getting by. We needed to make *extra* money so we could invest. We wanted to achieve financial independence, and we were suddenly alive to the possibility that the harder we worked, the sooner we could get there.

As a result, we worked with a renewed sense of purpose and with a much better attitude. The more effort we put into our jobs, the better we did, and that eventually translated into raises and promotions. Speaking for myself, I even came to like what I did for a living. Ironically, by the time I retired, I felt like I could have kept working quite happily – if not forever, at least for several more years. But by then we had so many other things we wanted to do in life that we knew we'd better get busy, so at the age of 43 we left full-time work behind and never looked back.

To get to that point yourself, you're going to need to work harder and with more purpose than you ever have before. Your long-term goal should be to save up enough money that your money can work for you so you don't have to. It takes time to build up a nest egg of sufficient size to make this possible, but once you do, you can get off the treadmill forever and get on with the rest of your life.

Having a clearly defined end-date for your working years changes your perspective on things. Your career becomes just one phase of your life, a phase you'd like to be able to look back on with a certain amount of pride and feel like you accomplished something useful during that period. This change in attitude can turn work into something more than just a chore and make it rewarding and occasionally (dare we say it?) even a pleasure.

Once you decide to retire early, you're working for yourself as much as you're working for the company you're employed by. So prepare mentally to work with a purpose for a set number of years and see what comes of it. Take on the hard assignments no one else wants. Put some energy into it and let your journey to early retirement – the hard work you do to get there – become part of your success story.

Buy Time

When you decide to retire early you're really deciding to buy time – time when you are on your own clock and not someone else's. Because your time is valuable, we think you should buy as much of it as possible by working hard for a concentrated number of years so you have more time to spend later on however you may choose.

It's no longer enough for you to make ends meet – you need to make them exceed. Your goal in your working years should be to create seed money that isn't earmarked for bills, groceries, mortgage payments, and all the other necessities of life. This seed money *could* be thrown to the winds (spent on stuff), or it could be planted and allowed to grow into something that could cast a whole lot of shade on your future. Which do you think we recommend?

If you could have a big house or an early retirement but not both, which would you choose? If you're like us, you'd choose the early retirement and to heck with the big house! "That's all your house is," jokes the comedian George Carlin, "it's a place to keep your stuff while you go out and get more stuff." We're all guilty of buying more than we should sometimes and so we laugh, but it's not such a laughing matter once you make the decision to retire early. Buying stuff and buying time are in direct competition for your hard-earned money, and the choices you make in this regard have a direct bearing on your future.

Too many material possessions can frankly be a burden, and they certainly subtract from how much time you can buy. As you approach retirement, there's a fair chance you'll be trying to *unburden* yourself of stuff so you can downsize to a smaller space, so do yourself a favor and don't overburden yourself to begin with. Keep your pack light as you travel through life and you'll be a happier camper. Live simply, stay lean, buy only what you need, and you'll make faster progress on the road to early retirement.

We're not advocating you put all your eggs in one basket and only live for the future. You should have fun and adventures along the way even while saving up for early retirement. You don't want to miss out on life today because you were too busy saving up for tomorrow. Stay balanced and remember it's a marathon, not a sprint. Pace yourself accordingly.

You get rich slowly by putting in many years of consistent effort, not by pushing so hard you make yourself or those around you unhappy. If you follow the suggestions in this book, you'll spread your investments over such an extended period of time that they won't cause undue stress. You'll keep your investments uncomplicated so they won't occupy your every waking moment, and you'll put them on autopilot so they'll essentially take care of themselves once you get them up and running.

The idea is to *have* a life while also planning for a better one.

When you first start down this path, few will believe you can do it. People will smile and nod when you tell them about your plans, but inside they may be thinking it's just talk. Do yourself a favor and prove them wrong. Make your dream come true through a thousand small actions and decisions you take from day to day over the course of years, all of which add up to building wealth slowly.

If you're lucky and live to a ripe old age, you could invest 15 years of time and triple or quadruple your investment with 45 to 60 years of financial freedom. Now that's what we would call a timely investment!

Dream Big

Nearly every weekend during our working years, Robin and I would take long walks in the Colorado mountains near where we lived, and more often than not the conversation would turn at some point to all the fun things we were going to do once we retired. Where we were going to travel, where we were going to live overseas, the adventures we were going to have. Those were good walks! Keeping the dream alive – talking about it and making it real to each other – made all the scrimping and saving seem worthwhile.

And it *was* worthwhile. Retiring early is not a pipe dream: it's achievable, and it really does give you the freedom to do what you love most. For us it means being able to travel for longer periods of time than the two or three weeks our full-time jobs used to allow. Now our trips can last as long as we want them to; we can immerse ourselves in another culture and get to know it from the inside out.

Early retirement also means we can pursue our own interests without particular regard to money. We can write, take photographs, and keep a travel website simply because we want to, not because we have to. We also love the fact that when a perfectly sunny day comes along unexpectedly in the middle of the "work week," we can abandon whatever plans we might have had and go for a hike when there are virtually no people on the trails and nature is at its best.

It's liberating to be able to make decisions about how to spend your time once money is no longer the primary driver. Doors open on a whole new world of possibilities:

- Volunteer and community work that would have been closed to you before because they didn't pay a salary.

- Personal projects like writing or painting that fulfill an internal desire to create but may never reward you financially.

- Outdoor or cultural pursuits that enrich your soul but not your pocketbook.

What matters most is being able to make your own choice each morning when you wake up – to have a say in how you spend your day – because time really is the ultimate limited resource.

So let yourself dream about what you'll do once you retire and are still young enough to pursue your dreams. Visualize yourself retired early, then read on to learn how to build the financial bridge to get you there.

Chapter 2.
The Specifics: How We Retired Early

Lt may help to have a concrete example of what we did during our investing years as a guide to what you may also be able to accomplish. We provide a lot of specifics in this chapter to allow you to make a reasonable judgment as to what may be possible in your own life when it comes to early retirement. You can extrapolate from our situation to yours, using the detailed information below as a kind of financial yardstick.

Annual Salaries

Let's start with this chart summarizing our annual salaries. A detailed table of salary information is provided in Appendix A.

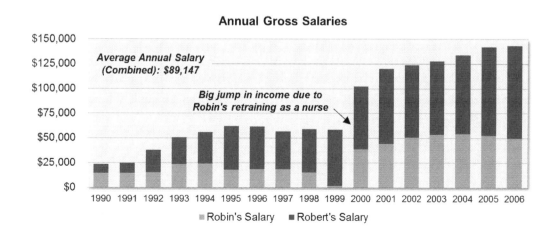

Annual Gross Salaries

Average Annual Salary (Combined): $89,147

Big jump in income due to Robin's retraining as a nurse

■ Robin's Salary　■ Robert's Salary

As the chart suggests, at first we were making very little money – less than $25,000 *combined* in 1990 and 1991. By 1992 we were up to $38,000. We had just purchased our home in November 1991 and weren't even officially saving for retirement yet. The beginnings of a meaningful investment plan didn't occur until late 1994. However, since our home ended up representing about one third of our net worth at retirement, we think it makes sense to start the retirement savings clock in 1992 just after we bought it.

For the first 8 years (from 1992 to 1999) we earned an average combined salary of just $55,000 gross. Our after-tax income averaged around $40,000. Out of this amount we had to pay a home mortgage ($1,050 per month), finish paying off car and college loans, and cover all the other typical bills and expenses that come with daily living. Investing on top of all this wasn't easy but we at least made a beginning, saving an average of about $8,900 per year during this period. We hope you will take some encouragement from this. It demonstrates you don't need a powerhouse salary to begin saving for early retirement. You can make a small start now, then work purposefully to improve your financial prospects over the course of your investing years.

Between 1999 and 2000 our income jumped dramatically due to Robin's retraining as a nurse. A quick glance at the chart shows what a powerful difference it can make having *two* good salaries working for you instead of just one. In the end, helped by Robin's new career and a reasonably strong finish in my own, our combined gross salaries averaged about **$89,000** for the 15 years from 1992 to 2006.

Let's look at one final salary statistic. Our combined gross salaries during our 12 primary investing years (from 1995 to 2006) averaged about **$99,000**. This is the financial yardstick that may be the most useful to you.

Based on this information, it's reasonable to assume a couple with no kids with combined salaries averaging **$100,000** gross per year could accomplish what we did or better. This should hold true even when taking inflation into account since our salary average over the entire 15-year period was actually under $90,000. If each of you earn $50,000, say, that would do the trick. The good news is, you don't need sky-high salaries to make this work, you simply need decent wages. Salaries in the $50,000 to $60,000 range are certainly attainable in the U.S. these days with a little retraining if necessary. Robin's second career as a nurse is a good case in point.

We believe a single individual saving for early retirement could achieve similar results with an average salary of about **$75,000**.

Parents earning $100,000 combined might need to tack on an extra 5 to 10 years to achieve financial independence due to the higher expenses associated with children. However, if your salaries average **$125,000** per year or more, you might be able to accomplish something similar to what we did even with kids.

Inflation tends to play havoc with hard numbers in books like these, so you may want to add 3% per year based on the book's publication date to translate the salary yardsticks listed above into current dollars.

Annual Investment Amounts

The following chart shows how much we invested each year for 15 years. (Exact amounts are provided in Appendix A.) This is what *we* invested, without reference to market returns or compounding.

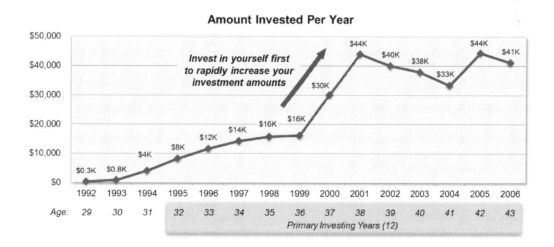

Amount Invested Per Year

You'll notice the dollar amounts start out small and grow much bigger with time. The arrow highlights the big jump in yearly savings (+$14,000) that occurred once Robin became a registered nurse in 2000. That amount jumped by another $14,000 in 2001 once we were done paying off over $15,000 in student nursing loans and could channel virtually all of the extra money she was earning straight into investments. The moral of the story is, invest in yourself first before investing for retirement if you want to maximize your results.

If you add up the total amount we put into investments from 1992 to 2006, it comes to just over $342,000. Again, this is the amount *we* put in, not counting market returns or compounding. That averages out to about **$22,800** in investments per year.

Keep in mind the first 3 years of this 15-year period were insignificant in terms of investing – our cumulative total from 1991 to 1994 was less than $6,600. At that point we were primarily focused on buying and furnishing our home, paying off loans, and switching to a 15-year mortgage. During our 12 primary years of investing (1995-2006), we averaged just over **$28,000** in investments per year.

Let's split the difference and say **$25,000** per year is a decent yardstick for an average annual investment amount (plus the equity building in your home) if you are aiming for early retirement in 15 years. Like us, though, your annual savings rate may start out much smaller than this. In our first 3 years we only saved about $1,750 per year on average, so don't be discouraged if $25,000 seems like an impossibly big number at the moment. With a 15- or 20-year plan, you have plenty of time to make career improvements to supercharge your savings.

Percentage of Net Income Invested

The next chart shows the percentage of our net income invested each year. As you can see, the percentages increased dramatically as the years passed.

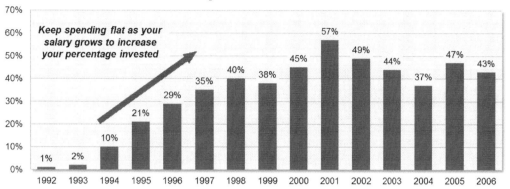

The percentage of our net income invested averages out to **33%** per year over 15 years, or **40%** per year during our 12 primary investing years (1995-2006). For yardstick purposes, if you're investing **one third** of your net income each year (and your salary is at least roughly comparable to ours), it's reasonable to assume you're on track to retire in about 15 years.

Over the years, we had to resist the natural tendency to spend more just because we were making more. Instead we directed any "bonus" money into investments. By keeping our expenses flat, we were able to save increasingly large amounts – especially after Robin's switch to a better-paying job. This took some self-discipline, but it made a world of difference in terms of the amounts we were able to invest each year. By making dozens of small cost-saving decisions each day – along with a few big ones like never moving from our starter home and keeping the same cars throughout our investing years – we were able to dramatically increase the gap between earning and spending in the later years of our plan.

Our investments as a percentage of net income hit an all-time high of 57% in 2001, then tailed off percentage-wise even though the dollar amounts invested continued to average around $40,000 per year. That's because we began living a bit more for today and a bit less for tomorrow at that point. By then our salaries were high enough and our money was working hard enough for us that we found it easier to reach our yearly goals without needing to sacrifice so much. We began traveling more after 2001, but we were still careful to pay ourselves first, making certain we could meet our yearly investing goals before venturing off on that next big trip.

Taxable vs. Tax-Advantaged Accounts

If you plan to retire very early like we did, you need to save at least some of your money in taxable accounts since tax-advantaged ones like 401(k)s and IRAs penalize you for withdrawing money before age 59½. As this chart indicates, we had to play catch-up investing in taxable accounts when we realized halfway through our investment plan we would be retiring earlier than expected and would need penalty-free access to more of our money.

At retirement we held almost $350,000 in taxable investments and $280,000 in tax-advantaged investments (a 55/45 split). Including the equity from the sale of our home ($200,000 of which was invested in a taxable bond fund at retirement), the split was closer to 65/35.

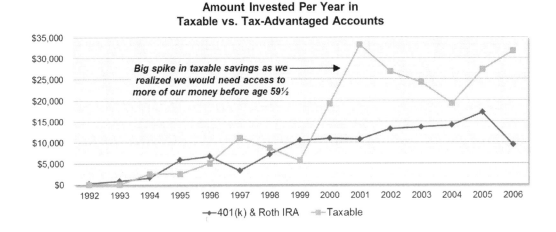

If you plan to retire in your thirties or forties, we think a good yardstick for the ratio of taxable to tax-advantaged savings is around **50/50**. If you expect to downsize like we did and put a portion of your home equity into taxable bonds, then aim for **60/40** inclusive of the bonds.

The closer you get to 59½ as your likely retirement age, the more it makes sense to put all or most of your savings into tax-advantaged accounts. There are ways to access money in your tax-advantaged accounts without penalty even before age 59½ (see "Allocating Between Taxable and Tax-Advantaged Accounts" in Chapter 12). If you plan to retire at age 55 or over, we recommend you max out your tax-advantaged savings options first before putting any money into taxable accounts.

Cumulative Nest Egg

This chart shows the cumulative nest egg we accrued over the 15-year period from 1992 to 2006. The nest egg shown is for liquid assets only and does not include equity in our home of about $300,000.

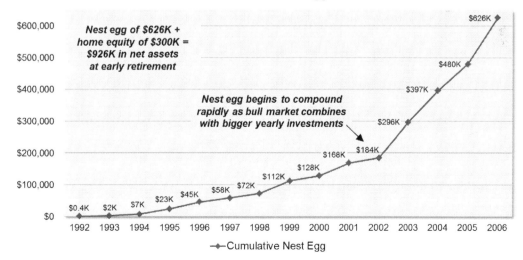

Cumulative Nest Egg

If you add up the total amount *we* put into investments from 1992 to 2006, it comes to just over $342,000 (as discussed earlier in this chapter under "Annual Investment Amounts"). Now compare this amount to the cumulative nest egg shown for 2006 of $626,000. The difference, which comes to about $284,000, is due to the effects of compounding. This is essentially your money working for you to earn more money, and it demonstrates what a powerful force compounding can be. Consider that about 45% of the total nest egg shown for 2006 is the result of compounding.

It's instructive to note that even though we were channeling large amounts of money into the markets from 2000 to 2002, our returns were unimpressive because the economy as a whole was in the midst of a significant bear market. The dot-com bubble had finally burst and the S&P 500 was down -9%, -12%, and -22% in 2000, 2001, and 2002. However, throughout the bear market we were buying *more shares* with our money and we knew that in the long run our strategy of consistent investing would pay off. And it did. We saw big returns in the following four years. From 2003 to 2006 the S&P 500 gained 29%, 11%, 5%, and 16%, respectively. Our cumulative nest egg grew rapidly under these conditions. Now the markets were working *for* us even as we continued channeling more money into them.

The takeaway lesson is this: keep investing – or invest more – when the markets are down and you will reap big rewards later on.

Even though the S&P 500 gained more percentage-wise in 2003 than it did in 2006 (29% vs. 16%), our individual returns were greater in 2006. Why? Because our capital base was greater: we had more money invested in the stock market by then. Think of it this way: If you have $5,000 invested in the stock market and the market has a banner 20% year, that's a gain of $1,000; but if you have $500,000 invested, you've just made yourself $100,000. Your dollar returns are typically much higher in the later years of your investment program. That's the nature of compounding, and it's why even a few extra years of work can make a big difference in terms of the size of your nest egg. If the markets cooperate, you can make impressive and rapid strides forward – and if they don't cooperate, at least any new money you're investing cushions your portfolio from going down as much as it would have otherwise. Your nest egg may even continue to increase slightly during a bear market, as ours did from 2000 to 2002.

Despite the compelling argument for staying in the workforce a few years longer and watching your nest egg grow bigger, the siren call of early retirement can sometimes be impossible to resist. Such was the case for us. After careful thought, we decided to quit full-time work two years earlier than planned and retire at age 43 instead of 45. We turned the page and started a new chapter in our lives.

Was it a good decision? As you turn the page yourself, we'll look at how things turned out for us once we left full-time work and ventured into the promised land of early retirement.

Chapter 3.
More Specifics: Life After Retirement

We retired earlier than originally planned because we didn't want to *almost* arrive at the promised land but not quite get there – like Moses leading his people through the desert for forty long years but being denied entry within sight of his goal. Robin's work as a nurse had taught her from personal experience life doesn't always go as planned. That reinforced our determination to retire as early as possible while both of us were still young and healthy enough to fully enjoy it.

So we took the plunge. It helped knowing one or both of us could always go back to work on a temporary basis if need be since both our jobs were suited to it. It also helped having a relatively high tolerance for risk and feeling more excited than scared at the thought of venturing into the unknown.

Then, too, when we looked at our portfolio balance, we felt like we had enough. Not a penny more, mind you, but enough. Only you can define what enough is for you, but in our case we had close to a million dollars saved up after selling our home, which was enough to generate about $40,000 in income per year. That was an amount we knew from experience we could live on comfortably.

A luxury retirement had never been our goal. From the beginning we wanted to save up just enough to be able to travel the world affordably and follow other pursuits of our own choosing like writing and photography. What we wanted more than money was *time*.

Some may be surprised we retired on less than a million dollars and think us foolhardy. Others may think we shortchanged ourselves by not putting in a few more years and saving up for a more deluxe retirement. Still others may think we waited too long and could have made the jump sooner. All we can say in response is that deciding when to retire is a deeply personal choice. What you decide may differ from what we decided, and that's fine. Part of the purpose of this book is to help you find *your* right balance between time and money, work and play, present and future.

Did we make the right decision? Did we jump at the right time? For us the answer is an unqualified yes. Even with 20/20 hindsight we would make the same decision again, and that's despite retiring right into the arms of the worst economic crisis since the Great Depression. We'll provide insights into how we weathered that financial storm towards the end of this chapter, but first let's take a look at some specifics to see what our financial picture looked like at the moment we retired.

Net Assets in Retirement

The following chart picks up where the Cumulative Nest Egg chart in the previous chapter left off. It shows our total net assets at retirement and beyond, including stocks, bonds, and real estate.

When we retired at the end of 2006, our *stock* holdings stood at about $587,000. They increased by $40,000 in 2007 before plummeting dramatically with the Great Recession. By year-end 2008 they had dropped by nearly 40% to just under $379,000, but by 2010 they had already recovered most of their lost ground.

Our *bond* holdings amounted to just under $300,000 in 2007 after we sold our home and invested the entire proceeds in a fund mirroring the total bond market. Abruptly we went from having a negligible bond position to a much larger one representing nearly a third of our portfolio. This was a much healthier portfolio balance for early retirees than a 100% stock portfolio would have been and was always part of our plan for early retirement. As the chart indicates, our bond fund held steady throughout the Great Recession – and in fact grew steadily, but we kept withdrawing dividends to live on so it stayed flat overall as a result.

Our *real estate* holdings began at $300,000, dropped to zero for two years, then remained at roughly $100,000 after 2008. After selling our home in 2007, we lived for

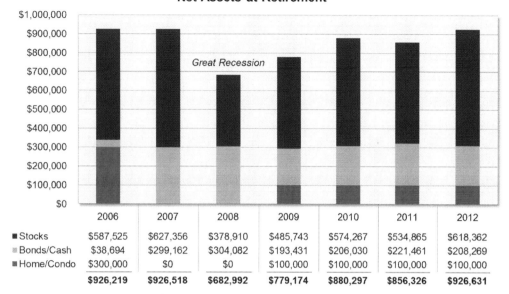

Net Assets at Retirement

	2006	2007	2008	2009	2010	2011	2012
■ Stocks	$587,525	$627,356	$378,910	$485,743	$574,267	$534,865	$618,362
▓ Bonds/Cash	$38,694	$299,162	$304,082	$193,431	$206,030	$221,461	$208,269
■ Home/Condo	$300,000	$0	$0	$100,000	$100,000	$100,000	$100,000
	$926,219	**$926,518**	**$682,992**	**$779,174**	**$880,297**	**$856,326**	**$926,631**

two years with no home at all, renting instead as we traveled. For those two years our assets were all liquid. In 2009, when real estate prices were near their lowest due to the housing crisis, we bought a small condo in Boulder for under $100,000, paying for it in cash with proceeds from our bond fund. The condo gives us a small place to call home when we're not on the road, plus a small foothold in the real estate market.

Just after selling our home in 2007, our investment portfolio stood at its all-time peak of $975,000. At that point we had about $350,000 in taxable stock funds, $300,000 in taxable bond funds, and $325,000 in tax-advantaged accounts that would remain off-limits and continue to grow undisturbed until we tapped into them some time after age 59½. The tax-advantaged accounts, consisting of my 401(k) plan and a Roth IRA for each of us, were 100% invested in stock index funds. All of our assets at that point were liquid, so our nest egg stood tantalizingly close to the $1 million mark in our first year of retirement.

From a purely financial perspective, it might have been wiser for us to work a bit longer until our liquid assets were worth $1 million *plus* another $100,000 to put towards some kind of real estate in the future. Slightly over **$1 million** is the yardstick we would recommend to you as the minimum amount for your nest egg going into retirement. One million dollars is a nice round sum of money, but it doesn't go as far as it once did, and it will go even less far due to the effects of inflation in future years. That amount can safely generate $40,000 per year, which is enough for a couple to live on at present if the couple is reasonably frugal by nature.

If you are very frugal or plan to live overseas in a less expensive country, you might be able to get by on even less. We think we could live on $30,000 per year if we didn't travel so intensively or spent most of our time living in a country where the dollar stretched further. We know other retired couples who get by on $30,000 or less – with travel of a more prudent nature included – who are quite happy with the lives they are living.

Billy and Akaisha Kaderli are a case in point. They retired at age 38 and run the highly useful website retireearlylifestyle.com. They are "perpetual travelers" who have lived on an average of $22,295 per year – or an average of $61.08 per day. They know this because they have carefully tracked their daily expenses every day since they retired in 1991.

If you visit Billy and Akaisha's website you will see they've had all sorts of adventures and have lived a very full life indeed on very little money. They are great examples of what is possible for all of us if we can only conquer our fears and take on the challenge of living life to the fullest. Their style of travel is to base themselves in a cost-friendly country like Mexico, Thailand, or Guatemala and stay longer than we typically do – often for years at a time. That approach makes their travel lifestyle more affordable and their experiences all the richer.

If you expect to supplement your retirement income with some kind of part-time work or semi-retirement option, that can also reduce the size of the nest egg you need, as discussed towards the end of this chapter.

Investment Mix at Retirement

The two pie charts show how our investments were roughly allocated before and after retirement.

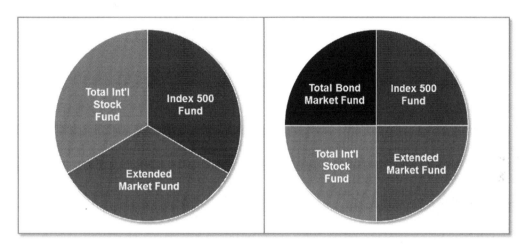

We were virtually 100% invested in stocks while saving up for retirement, but we shifted to a mix of 70% stocks and 30% bonds upon retiring and selling our home. Shortly thereafter, we found ourselves grateful for every percent we had invested in bonds, because they remained stable during the Great Recession even while stocks plummeted. After purchasing our condo for $100,000 in 2009 using proceeds from our bond fund, our portfolio mix shifted closer to 75% stocks and 25% bonds and has remained in the 25-30% range ever since.

As a yardstick for you once you retire, we would recommend a stock-to-bond portfolio mix of:

- **70/30** if you are an aggressive investor
- **60/40** if you are a middle-of-the-road investor
- **50/50** if you are a conservative investor

A continued strong presence in stocks is important because stocks have the greatest potential for growth over the long term and give you the best chance of staying ahead of inflation.

We continue to believe an 80% to 100% investment in stocks or stock mutual funds makes sense while you are fully employed and actively saving for retirement, but your needs change dramatically once you're retired and begin drawing down your investments on a regular basis.

At present we find ourselves reluctant to lessen our position in stocks because they seem poised to make strong gains as the economy mends and money flows back into the markets. We'd like to see our net assets cross the million-dollar threshold for the first time, and we believe stocks offer the best potential to get us there. That said, we do consider ourselves slightly overweighted in stocks at present. As they continue to move higher, we hope to gradually rebalance our portfolio to increase our safety net and move closer to the 70/30 (or perhaps even 60/40) stock-to-bond mix we've suggested to you as being ideal once you're in retirement mode.

Annual Withdrawals Since Retirement

Since this is a book about retiring early on less, it won't surprise you we try to keep our expenses as low as reasonably possible in retirement. During our six years of retirement so far, we have lived on **$40,000 per year**, or an average of about **$3,300 per month**. That amount includes all living expenses, travel expenses, credit card bills, and so on. The following table shows our annual withdrawals since retiring, including the source of each withdrawal.

Our two biggest recurring monthly expenses at present are catastrophic health insurance premiums ($350 total at age 49/50) and our condo HOA fee ($200). Other recurring expenses like cell phone service, basic cable and internet, and gas/electric average less than $50 each per month. Car insurance and property taxes also average out to less than $50 per month.

We keep a single primary credit card and use it for everything from travel to fuel, groceries to takeout, and bricks-and-mortar purchases to Amazon purchases. We do not track expenses or keep a monthly budget per se any more, although we did so for a period of time until it became second nature for us to keep one eye on

Year	Date	Source	Withdrawal Amount
2007	Jan 4	Vanguard Intermediate-Term Bond Fund	$10,000
	Apr 2	Vanguard Intermediate-Term Bond Fund	$10,000
	Jul 10	Vanguard Intermediate-Term Bond Fund	$10,000
	Oct 1	Other*	$9,500
2008	Jan 1	Vanguard Total International Stock Fund	$15,000
	Apr 28	Company Stock	$15,000
	Aug 25	Vanguard Total Bond Market Fund	$10,000
2009	Jan 2	Vanguard Total Bond Market Fund	$15,000
	May 19	Vanguard Total Bond Market Fund	$10,000
		Part-Time Consulting Work	*$15,000*
2010		*Part-Time Consulting Work*	*$40,000*
2011		*Part-Time Consulting Work*	*$10,000*
	Jan 7	Company Stock	$20,000
	Aug 16	Vanguard Intermediate-Term Bond Fund	$10,000
2012	Jan 6	Vanguard Total Bond Market Fund	$10,000
	Feb 28	Vanguard Total Bond Market Fund	$10,000
	May 23	Vanguard Total Bond Market Fund	$10,000
	Aug 24	Vanguard Intermediate-Term Bond Fund	$500
	Sep 24	Company Stock	$9,500
Total Withdrawn from All Funds (Stocks & Bonds)			$165,000
Total from Part-Time Consulting Salary (net 6 mo.)			$65,000
Total from Other Sources (PERA + Rent)			$9,500
Grand Total (2007-2012)			$239,500
Average Per Year (All Sources)			**$39,916**
Average Per Year (Stocks & Bonds Only)			**$27,500**

*$7,350 net from PERA (nurse retirement account) cashed out;
$2,150 net from 5-mo. home rental (prior to home sale)*

expenses at all times. We do budget on a yearly basis, and we have been careful to stay within our self-imposed yearly limit thus far. We have not needed to adjust for inflation so far but may find it necessary to do so eventually.

Our preferred norm is to withdraw $10,000 per quarter, which makes it easy to gauge whether we're on track for the year. We usually withdraw money from whichever fund is performing the best at the moment. We can rebalance our portfolio to some degree simply by taking from whatever fund has performed best of late. Rebalancing a taxable account always has tax consequences, so we try to minimize our rebalancing efforts to these types of withdrawals.

Our primary source of withdrawals over the past six years was our investments: $165,000 total, or $27,500 per year on average. A second important source was a short-term consulting job I took during the depths of the Great Recession. I earned approximately $65,000 net during a six-month period, which was enough to fund 1½ years' worth of retirement living without our having to draw down our investments during an extremely difficult period in the markets. We'll talk more about part-time work and semi-retirement at the end of this chapter.

With stocks and stock mutual funds, it is always our goal to buy low and sell high, and of course that should be your goal as well. If we can't sell high, then we rely instead on a different stock fund that is performing better, or else on the dividends and interest from our bond fund. During the Great Recession, for example, the stock of the company for which I once worked continued to perform well enough that we were able to sell shares of it in 2008 and 2011 when it was at or near its all-time highs. Similarly, we sold shares of Vanguard Total International Stock Fund in January 2008 when it was at or near its all-time high.

Most investment withdrawals since retirement have been from our bond funds, which have served as our workhorses over the past six years. At first we used the Vanguard Intermediate-Term Bond Fund, relying on it essentially as our cash fund. During 2006 (the year before we retired), we ploughed $30,000 into this fund, knowing we would need access to ready cash over the coming year.

Eventually we switched to using the Vanguard Total Bond Market Index Fund both as our primary bond savings vehicle and as our "cash fund." We have kept the principal amount essentially steady and have used the dividends it generates for living expenses. The bond fund provides much better rates of return than our bank checking account would. The fund's average annual return since inception has been 6.7%.

It's easy to electronically transfer money out of the Vanguard bond funds to our Wells Fargo checking account. The process only takes two or three business days, and it is so reliable we no longer feel the need to keep a separate emergency fund since we know we can access this money so easily in a pinch. Since the bond fund generates dividends on a monthly basis, it tends to replenish itself in a reliable manner.

We keep our bank holdings to a minimum and have just a simple checking account. We have no savings account, CDs, or money markets. Bank rates are so low in the current economic climate that we find them unattractive for anything other than parking the cash we anticipate needing over the next two or three months.

While $40,000 is the amount we feel comfortable living on each year, it may not be the right amount for you. Part of the purpose of this book is to help you decide what your yardstick for annual withdrawals should be. In Chapter 8 ("Determine Your Retirement Income Needs"), we walk you step by step through the process of how to estimate your yearly expenses in retirement based on your current living expenses, which in turn can help you determine the size of the nest egg you'll need.

Income Taxes in Retirement

The following table lists the annual income taxes we paid from 1990 to 2012, including all federal, state, social security, and Medicare taxes. You'll notice there's quite a difference in the percentage of income taxes paid before and after retirement. Before retirement our average annual income tax as a percentage of gross salary was 25%. After retirement we typically paid $0 in income taxes. Even when you include the temporary consulting assignment I worked, the average income tax over six years of retirement still comes out to less than 9%.

The table illustrates how precipitously income taxes can drop once you are no longer earning wages. For example, in our final working years we were paying nearly $40,000 per year in income taxes – which is the same annual amount we are able to *live* on in retirement. In 2009 and 2010 we once again paid income taxes due to the

Year	Gross Salaries (Combined)	Total Income Taxes	Percentage Paid in Taxes
1990	$23,452	$4,740	20.2%
1991	$24,594	$5,973	24.3%
1992	$38,005	$7,509	19.8%
1993	$50,659	$10,828	21.4%
1994	$55,928	$12,523	22.4%
1995	$62,084	$15,963	25.7%
1996	$61,685	$14,471	23.5%
1997	$56,880	$12,948	22.8%
1998	$59,096	$12,714	21.5%
1999	$58,719	$14,279	24.3%
2000	$102,292	$32,123	31.4%
2001	$120,240	$36,044	30.0%
2002	$123,867	$34,831	28.1%
2003	$127,981	$33,847	26.4%
2004	$133,859	$35,952	26.9%
2005	$142,403	$39,237	27.6%
2006	$143,513	$39,374	27.4%
Early Retirement			
2007		$0	0%
2008		$0	0%
2009	$21,805*	$5,197*	23.8%
2010	$68,600*	$19,556*	28.5%
2011		$0	0%
2012		$0	0%

Income from 6-month aerospace consulting job

six-month consulting assignment I took on, which just goes to show that salary and taxes tend to go hand in hand.

It comes down to this: if you're planning a simple early retirement, you stand a good chance of paying much lower income taxes than you've become accustomed to in your working years. You may want to factor that into your retirement planning.

While your income tax may not always be zero in retirement, it could quite conceivably be 10% or less.

This is good news if you're thinking of retiring early on less: not only do you get out of the rat race sooner, you also get to reduce your income taxes sooner.

Dividend Income in Retirement

Let's take a look at one particular year to get a sense of how income taxes work in retirement, especially with regard to dividends and capital gains. In 2008 we had no income from wages. Instead our income was based solely on withdrawals from taxable investments: $15,000 from Vanguard Total International Stock Fund, $15,000 from company stock, and $10,000 from Vanguard Total Bond Market Fund.

The bond fund generated about $1,200 per month in dividends in 2008, or $14,500 per year. We initially assumed we would take quite a tax hit from that. However, since our bond income was no longer being added on top of earned income from a salary, it no longer had the same tax consequences it would have had during our working years.

Instead, this dividend income was more than offset by the IRS's standard deductions and exemptions for a married couple filing jointly (totaling $17,900 in 2008). Thus the IRS standard deductions and exemptions can be used as a sort of benchmark: if your dividends stay at or below this benchmark, then you should owe no taxes on such income.

Capital Gains in Retirement

In that same year our capital gains totaled $17,196. However, from 2008 to 2012, qualified dividends and long-term capital gains were taxed at 0% if you fell within the 15% tax bracket or below. Part of the reason we sold company stock in 2008 was to take advantage of this 0% rate since we knew our company stock had appreciated more than any other asset we owned.

It's important to remember that you never owe taxes on the cost basis of the money you put into stocks, bonds, and mutual funds. So when we took $15,000 out of our International Stock fund, for example, we didn't have $15,000 in capital gains because about $9,800 of that amount was cost basis (money we put in). The other $5,200 represented the long-term capital gains we had realized, and that was the amount we *would* have owed taxes on if our long-term capital gains tax rate hadn't been zero.

With the company stock, only about $3,000 of the $15,000 was cost basis, so we would have owed taxes on $12,000 of capital gains in a "non-zero" tax year.

With our bond fund, $9,988 of the $10,000 we withdrew was cost basis, so we only would have owed taxes on about $12 of capital gains. The bond fund had barely appreciated at all from a capital gains standpoint, although it did generate plenty of dividends as discussed above.

Retiring Into Recession

"If you didn't lose a lot of money during the Panic of 2008, you were probably doing something wrong," write Ben Stein and Philip DeMuth in *The Little Book of Bulletproof Investing.*

Well, apparently we weren't doing anything wrong. We lost plenty over the short term, and we weren't the only ones. The Federal Reserve recently released numbers indicating the wealth of the average American family plunged 40% from 2007 to 2010.

The Great Recession certainly tested the two of us financially in ways we never could have imagined heading into early retirement, but we also found ways to weather the storm and even prosper over the long run. Here's a brief account of how we retired into severe recession. We learned some important lessons along the way and would like to share them with you here.

Where We Stood Pre-Recession

During our first year of retirement in 2007, just before the Great Recession, we lived on just under $40,000 and saw our net worth hold steady, even with the five-month trip we had taken to New Zealand and Fiji. We took that as a good sign: our investments were earning enough to keep up with our withdrawals. We were doing exactly what we had hoped to do: living off the earnings from our investments while the underlying capital remained intact and even continued to grow.

On October 9, 2007, the Dow stood at its all-time high at the time of 14,164.53 and our personal portfolio stood at its all-time high of just over $975,000. We were starting to flirt with the idea of crossing the million dollar threshold for the first time and naturally felt excited about it – but it wasn't to be.

The Recession Strikes

During the rest of 2007 and into 2008 the markets slid slowly but relentlessly downward. Then in September 2008 the bottom fell out. Lehman Brothers went bankrupt and all the other dominoes began to fall.

We watched in dismay as, over the next several months, our portfolio shrank in spectacular fashion. Our net worth went from $975,000 in October 2007 to $683,000 by the end of 2008. The carnage continued into 2009 when our portfolio hit its low point of $592,000 on March 9. Meanwhile the Dow had dropped to a new low of 6,547 – 53.8% lower than its October 2007 high.

Our portfolio was down nearly $400,000 from its high point. That nearly 40% loss would have been even worse if we had been 100% invested in the stock market, but fortunately we had invested the $300,000 from the sale of our home into a bond fund mirroring the total bond market. That fund stayed stable and even went up in value. Suddenly we found our bond holdings represented more than 50% of our portfolio value simply because our stock fund valuations had sunk so low.

The bond fund was our silver lining during that turbulent time. It provided us with at least one source from which we could withdraw money without feeling distraught.

Paper Losses

As for our stock funds, they were terribly beaten up, but we knew as long as we didn't sell shares of those funds, the losses were only paper losses. That is to say, the losses weren't locked in unless we actually sold shares of any of our stock funds, and we were determined not to do that.

To put it another way, we still had the same number of *shares* in our stock funds as we had when the markets were at their all-time highs – it's just that each share had less value. If we were patient enough and waited until share valuations increased again, our paper losses would be erased.

And indeed, after the March 2009 lows, stocks rallied and share valuations increased dramatically during the rest of the year. By 2009 our net worth at year's end stood at $780,000, and by 2010 we stood at $880,000. That was still $45,000 down from the 2007 year-end close, but nevertheless that was a heck of a lot better than being $400,000 down.

Treading Water

The main reason our portfolio recovered so well during this period was because we withdrew very little money from it. I took a temporary consulting job for six months, which provided us with a cash cushion that helped us ride out the storm until the markets recovered. In essence we treaded water, making just enough so we didn't have to take from our investments while the markets were at their worst.

In the next section we talk in more detail about part-time work and semi-retirement, but for now suffice it to say that staying flexible and pragmatic in early retirement can be an important attribute when you're faced with the unexpected.

No Buffer for Poor Market Returns

One important lesson we learned from the Great Recession was that once you enter retirement and start living off your investments, you are much more reliant on market performance than ever before. You have no new money going into the markets to buffer the effects of poor returns.

You also lose the psychological benefit that comes from investing new money into the markets during a downturn. You can no longer say, "Well, at least I'm buying new shares on sale at a low price," because you're no longer buying new shares. If anything, you're having to sell shares to cover living expenses.

Technically speaking, you could rearrange your existing portfolio to put more money into stocks, but it's awfully hard to take money out of a bond fund that's providing you with your sole reliable source of income and put it into stocks in the midst of a volatile market. Not only would you be reducing your income stream at exactly the wrong moment, but you'd also be increasing your risk.

Even if you were to take on a temporary job to tide you over until the markets recovered (as we did), you'd likely need whatever money you were earning just to live on and wouldn't be able to invest it in the stock market no matter how good the opportunities might look.

When Bad News Is Good News

Until we retired, we had always welcomed bad news in the markets. Why? Because bad news is actually good news for beginning and middle-years investors. Bad news spells opportunity. This may seem counterintuitive but it makes perfect sense once you think about it. If you had bought stocks in March 2009, for instance, when the Dow stood at around 6,500, you would have been participating in an amazing 50% off sale. If you could buy the latest iPhone for half off, wouldn't you think it was a great deal and rush out to buy it? And yet we don't always bring that same logic to our investments.

As a beginning investor, your time horizon is so long that you should be excited about bad financial news. It means you get to buy more shares for less money. If stock prices stayed depressed for another decade, that would be fine from your standpoint. Bear markets are like extended sales at your favorite store: scoop up as many deals as you can while the getting is good.

Likewise, while it might be psychologically challenging to watch your investments soar and plummet repeatedly, such volatility has no real effect on the beginning or middle-years investor. All that really matters is where your investments stand when you cash them out. If the stock market goes on a major bull run in the last five years of your investment plan, all those shares you purchased at low, low prices are suddenly going to bear remarkable fruit.

So for beginning and middle-years investors our advice is simple: keep investing. Keep telling yourself the markets *have* to go up eventually. If you have a 15- to 20-year time horizon, you're almost certain to be proven right.

When Bad News Really Is Bad News

For endgame investors and retirees, bad news really is bad news. Both gains *and* losses are magnified. If the markets suddenly lose 20% and you have $500,000 invested in the stock market, that's a $100,000 loss you have to stomach (at least on paper).

Nor do you have the luxury of a long time horizon in which to recover. As a new retiree you need access to at least some of your money *now*. If stocks plunge, you won't feel happy about having to sell them at a deep loss just to pay the bills. It's for this very reason that a bond fund becomes crucial once you retire.

Safe Havens for Retirees

If there's one lesson we learned from the Great Recession, it's that saving for retirement and being retired are two very different animals. While saving for retirement, we recommend you invest aggressively in stock index funds. But as you near retirement, your needs change dramatically and you become at least as interested in protecting the capital you already have as you are in making more of it.

For this reason we recommend you have a bond index fund once you retire that represents at least 25% of your portfolio and preferably more. A 30% stake would be wiser, and 40% or even 50% isn't out of the question if you consider yourself a more conservative investor.

If you are willing to downsize once you retire, the equity from your home can make for a perfect transfusion of cash into a bond fund. The equity in your primary home is tax-free up to $250,000 per individual or $500,000 per couple. Take that money and put it into a bond fund so the capital remains safe and hopefully continues to grow. Our Vanguard Total Bond Market Index Fund, for example, has returned 6.7% on average since inception, which isn't half bad for a relatively safe investment.

Two other safe havens worth mentioning are TIPS bond funds and precious metals funds. Treasury Inflation-Protected Securities, or TIPS, have inflation protection built into them and are backed by the full faith and credit of the U.S. government. If a day ever comes when high inflation rears its ugly head again, TIPS should offer retirees a safe port in the storm.

For the same reason, a small position in a precious metals fund – if bought at reasonable valuations – is worth considering because such funds tend to run counter to the markets. They provide you with a small pool from which you can drink until the drought ends and the rest of your portfolio has time to heal.

Part-Time Work and Semi-Retirement

There is never a good time for a severe recession, but the worst time, experts say, is right after you retire because you can end up depleting your capital faster than you expected. Your nest egg can take a dramatic hit during a severe and extended downturn in the economy and never fully recover. We certainly didn't want that to happen after having worked so hard to reach the point where we could retire early.

Instead, we wanted to do all we could to minimize our withdrawals until market conditions improved.

So when the Great Recession hit and we realized it wouldn't be ending any time soon, we began to consider our options. Either we could tighten our belts – really tighten them – to the point where we were taking out the minimum possible amount to live on until the markets recovered, or we could earn a little money on the side so we didn't have to withdraw from our portfolio during a troubling time.

The belt-tightening option had its appeal, especially if we could do it in a foreign country where our dollar would stretch further and we could enjoy new experiences at the same time. We were actively considering such an option when a different kind of opportunity came knocking at our door.

When Opportunity Knocks

In the end the decision practically made itself. Out of the blue I was offered a temporary consulting assignment at an aerospace firm within easy driving distance of our condo. It was for a big proposal effort that was right up my alley. The assignment was only expected to last three months, which was perfect as far as I was concerned. I took the job and considered myself fortunate.

Of course, as often happens with proposals, the assignment ended up lasting longer than expected, so instead of three months I wound up working six (from September 2009 to February 2010). But that six months provided us with enough cash for nearly two years' worth of retirement living – including an expensive trip to Italy and Switzerland (with a cruise to Greece and Turkey thrown in for good measure). That splurge trip was our 25th wedding anniversary gift to each other, and it wouldn't have been possible without the temporary work I had done.

Interestingly enough, the consulting assignment turned out to be the best work experience of my life. The very fact that it was temporary made all the difference. I enjoyed getting to do something I was good at on my own terms. For that short window of time I put my whole heart and soul into winning the proposal effort (which we did, by the way) – and then it was done. The very next day Robin and I jetted off to India and Nepal for an unforgettable three-month trip. In no time at all the work assignment faded away like a pleasant but distant dream.

Now, we might have been able to live on minimum withdrawals from our investments – say, $25,000 per year – with some serious belt tightening, but we certainly wouldn't have been able to go on an extended trip to Europe without the help of that temporary salary. So you may want to think twice before dismissing out of hand the thought of a little part-time work in retirement.

In the Driver's Seat

Part-time work can go a long way towards padding a nest egg that's not quite as healthy as you'd like, or it can give you splurge money to do something you might not let yourself do otherwise. Any money you earn goes straight into your pocket instead of being invested, so even a little can make a big difference. We think it's a better solution than fretting about finances or feeling strapped for cash unnecessarily.

It's important to remember no one is holding a gun to your head once you retire and saying you *can't* work. These days it's all up to you what you want your retirement to be. As Fred Brock writes in *Retire on Less Than You Think,* "Retirement is becoming a time not when we stop work, but when we work at what we love – on our own terms."

We couldn't agree more. Financial independence puts you in the driver's seat when it comes to work. You can take it or leave it depending on how you feel. Speaking for myself, I remain open to future work assignments of two to three months, although so far the only notable work either of us has done in six years of retirement has been that one proposal assignment.

Taking a more flexible approach to retirement frankly makes it less frightening to retire early. Instead of all or nothing, there is the enticing possibility of something in between. It's not so scary taking the plunge if you know you have a lifeline waiting for you just in case you should need it. Certainly we find it comforting knowing that if things get tight, Robin can work a short-term nursing stint or I can take on another temporary proposal assignment. Or we could go in a completely different direction and work for a smaller amount of money in a foreign country but at something that would bring us pleasure anyway. Just consider the following three opportunities.

Tempting Overseas Assignments

Willing Workers On Organic Farms (WOOFF) offers tempting work assignments all over the world in exchange for your part-time labor harvesting grapes or feeding chickens or learning how to make goat cheese. Hey, why not? If you have an interest in organic farming anyway, or simply think it sounds cool to try your hand at something different, then you could learn a lot while also helping someone else out. Plus you'll get to know the locals in a way you never would have otherwise, while also visiting a part of the world you're curious about anyway.

The Caretaker Gazette (caretaker.org) offers caretaking assignments all over the U.S. and the world, from watching someone's pet to temporarily running a B&B to straightforward housesitting requests. We're subscribers and have taken on a handful of caretaking opportunities ourselves. We've seen undemanding opportunities on offer in England, France, Italy, Australia, the Caribbean, Belize, all fifty U.S. states, and many more tempting locales. Some assignments are for money but most are for lodging in exchange for simple work. Caretaking can make your travels abroad very inexpensive and can let you fit in with the local community in a way the typical traveler doesn't normally get to experience.

Teaching English abroad has already become something of a time-honored tradition for Americans who want to do more than just visit a country for a week. If you love the thought of teaching kids or adults something you already know by heart anyway – that is, your own native tongue –why not consider it? This can be an especially good option in countries that otherwise would be expensive to visit, such as Japan or Taiwan or certain countries in the Middle East. Wherever you decide to do your teaching, it can afford you a decent salary (compared to the local cost of living), free or inexpensive accommodation, and reimbursement for your plane ticket, not to mention the opportunity for cultural immersion and region-wide travel.

The Appeal of Semi-Retirement

Semi-retirement is a particularly compelling option for those whose retirement savings aren't quite as robust as they'd like them to be. We've met many expats in foreign countries who are running their own businesses – small cafes catering to Americans who miss burritos and pizza, for example – to supplement meager retirement savings or social security checks. They put in a few hours of work a day during the lunch or dinner hour in exchange for getting to live in an interesting part of the world while also participating in local community life.

You can semi-retire sooner than you can fully retire, which is an important benefit in its own right. Your nest egg can be smaller because it only has to fund a portion of your retirement. A minimal amount of work can fund the rest. Whether you choose to work just a few hours each day or carve out a few months each year and have the rest of the year to yourself is up to you, but either approach can get you to your goal of greater freedom in a shorter amount of time.

Semi-retirement also appeals to those who are worried about being bored or having too much time on their hands. "Fully 80% of Americans between the ages of 40 and 58 expect to work in retirement," writes Bob Clyatt in *Work Less, Live More*. "While a third of those expect to need the income, two-thirds – or fully half of the Baby Boom generation – say they are interested in rotating between leisure and work during retirement as a way to keep mentally challenged and active."

Work instantly becomes less onerous once it's mixed in with breaks – preferably long breaks in our opinion! Working a few months a year at something you enjoy anyway is hardly a burden, and it can balance nicely with a lifestyle of travel and cultural exploration. Working in short bursts can be a pleasure, and more and more retirees are thinking of retirement in just such a way. If this approach appeals to you, then put semi-retirement on your radar screen as a possibility in your future.

Semi-retirement offers a way to dip your toes into the retirement waters and see if they are to your liking. It can offer a nice transition into full-time retirement, or it can become your modus operandi for years to come. It's your choice.

Chapter 4.
Your Roadmap to Early Retirement

Our goal in the next ten chapters is to provide you with practical advice on how to get from Point A to Point B – from full-time work to financial independence – in the least amount of time and with a minimum of fuss and detours. In essence Chapters 5 to 14 constitute a roadmap to early retirement that you can follow step by step to get to your destination.

Take the Highway

Sometimes it just makes sense to take the highway and avoid all the stoplights and traffic on local roads. In similar fashion, you want to make sure you get onto the financial highway as early as possible and stay there until you reach your exit. That means investing primarily in stocks and stock mutual funds, not cash or bonds, during most of your investing years. Why? Because stocks *are* the highway: they offer the fastest, most direct, and most reliable way to get to your goal.

You also want to make sure your vehicle – which is to say your career – is up to the task of getting you there. Don't get onto the highway in a clunker and find you can't keep up – or worse yet, break down by the side of the road. Instead, purchase a reliable car (a practical career) first and save yourself a whole lot of trouble on the road ahead.

Avoid Shortcuts

Short cuts make for long delays, as the saying goes. Trying to take too many shortcuts on the road to early retirement can end up backfiring on you. By shortcuts we mean any high-risk investment aimed at getting rich quick rather than getting rich slowly. Day trading, currency trading, options trading, investing in hedge funds, investing in risky stocks, going all-in on the next big thing, investing in financial products you don't really understand, and investing in anything that seems too good to be true all fall under the category of shortcuts to be avoided if you're following a get rich slowly approach.

We don't mean to imply there's anything wrong with getting rich quick if you can do it reliably, but it's not what this book is about. Plenty of other books cover that topic. Getting rich quick is a bit like bobbing and weaving through traffic to get to your destination just as fast as you can, whereas getting rich slowly is more like driving on the highway but staying in the middle lane. It may not be wind-in-your-hair exhilarating, but it offers a relatively safe and predictable way of getting you to your goal.

Milestones Along Your Route

Here is a preview of what's coming down the pike. The first milestone on your route is entitled "Invest in Yourself First" (Chapter 5), and it comes first for a reason. Without a reliable career, everything else about your journey becomes more difficult.

The next milestone is "Get Out of Debt" (Chapter 6), and it comes second for a reason too. We'll explain why we recommend you pay off all credit cards, car loans, and college loans first before beginning to invest in earnest for retirement.

The next six milestones are all dedicated to the specifics of how to invest successfully for early retirement:

- How to use compounding to your advantage (Chapter 7)
- How to calculate your likely income needs in retirement (Chapter 8)
- How to determine the size of the nest egg you'll need (Chapter 9)
- How to put together a personalized investment plan (Chapter 10)
- How to put your index fund investments on auto-pilot (Chapter 11)
- How to allocate between 401(k), IRA, and taxable accounts (Chapter 12)

Are we there yet? Not quite. There are two more milestones along your route, both of them having to do with how to keep your expenses low so you can retire sooner and stay retired on less. It's frankly hard to find a retirement book out there that doesn't have a chapter devoted to the subject of living below your means (Chapter 13). Why? Because it's probably the single most important thing you can do to reach early retirement and stay retired. "Live below your means" might seem like overly obvious advice, but obvious doesn't always equate with easy to implement in real life. We provide practical guidance on how to put this advice into practice. The last roadmap chapter (Chapter 14) provides further details on how to keep two of your biggest expenses in life –home and cars – as low as reasonably possible.

After that it's about time for a rest stop. "Keep Your Life Portfolio Balanced" (Chapter 15) reminds you to balance living for today with living for tomorrow lest you run out of energy along the way.

The final two chapters in the book cover subjects of particular interest to those who have already reached their destination. How to pay for health care has always been a concern for just about anyone who has ever considered retiring early. In "Health Care in Retirement" (Chapter 16), we share good news about the Affordable Care Act in America and medical tourism overseas, both of which bode well for early retirees on a budget.

We finish up with a chapter on extended travel in retirement (Chapter 17). Here we offer suggestions on how to keep your travel costs down as you head off on journeys the likes of which you could only dream about during your working years. Since long-term travel is both the motivation and the reward for many early retirees, we think this makes for a fitting and fun final chapter.

Chapter 5.
Invest in Yourself First

By the age of 31 Robin and I only had a total of about $6,500 invested for retirement, and that was primarily in my 401(k) at work. It was a start but we wanted to do more – a lot more. We wanted to accelerate our savings. But how? We had very little fat left to trim out of our budget. What we needed wasn't a way to cut expenses more but a way to make more money.

"I should probably find out what I'm worth in the business marketplace now that I've got three years of experience under my belt," I wrote in my journal around that same time. "Increasing my salary would be the quickest way to speed us along on our financial highway."

Yes! Now you're talking, younger me.

It took me longer than most people, but I was finally waking up to the fact that I had to make strides in my career if I ever wanted my early retirement dreams to be more than just dreams. It would take us another five years before we realized that Robin, too, needed to switch careers and retrain as a nurse. Call us slow learners, but eventually we came to the conclusion that *we are our own best investments*. Hopefully you can learn this lesson sooner than we did and profit from it.

Why Minimum Wage Won't Work

If you find you're barely able to make ends meet with the salary you're currently making, we advise you to invest in yourself first before doing any other investing. Working a low-wage job won't get you where you want to go fast enough. To retire early you have to live *below* your means so you can invest any extra money and start building up a capital base. How can you do that if it takes every cent you have just to get by?

The federal minimum wage is currently $7.25 per hour. Assuming a forty-hour work week, that's $15,000 per year. That's barely enough for most people to survive on in the U.S. these days. It doesn't give you the wherewithal to put sufficient money aside to allow for an early retirement. You may be the hardest worker in the world, but if you're in a field that pays low wages, you're going to find it hard going at best. So instead we suggest you put your hard work ethic to work on yourself first.

Choosing a Practical Career

Investing in yourself first means getting an education in something *practical* that you know ahead of time will pay well once you graduate. The education may be expensive, but if you know there are attractive jobs that pay well and are in high demand on the other side of that education, it will be worth every penny you spend on it and more to make it happen.

The education we're talking about isn't necessarily a four-year degree at a college or university. It *could* be that if you have a specific career in mind that expressly requires it. But before you go down such a long and financially arduous path, make sure there is a strong demand for workers in that field, that the only individuals who can fill such jobs are people with the education you're about to get, and that the jobs pay highly enough to justify such a prolonged effort.

Otherwise, there are many careers that pay reasonably well but call for a more focused set of courses that can be completed in a year or two. Think LPN in the nursing field (or RN if you already have a college degree); EMT or paramedic; dental hygienist; loan officer; paralegal; technical writer; executive assistant; police officer; plumber or electrician; auto mechanic; real estate agent; customs officer; security alarm installer; HVAC technician; sales representative; etc. Do some brainstorming and web surfing to get ideas flowing as you consider a wide range of possible career choices.

Don't be afraid to think outside the box. For instance, you might consider the possibility of going to a trade school, or starting your own business, or running a franchise, or becoming an entrepreneur. You may want to focus your attention on fields in which humans aren't likely to be replaced by computers any time soon. The classic example is nursing.

You don't need to become a doctor or a lawyer or earn an outrageously high salary to retire early, but you do need to have a decent job paying a decent wage – say, in the $50,000 range. If you're earning $30,000 or less and have little hope of making more, you should consider a career change because otherwise you're making it harder on yourself than it has to be.

The career you choose doesn't have to be your all-time dream career. It should certainly be something you don't *hate* doing because you're going to have to do it for awhile – probably 15 years or more. It would be vastly preferable to like what you do, but it's some comfort to remember you aren't wedded to your job for life but only until you retire early.

Biting the Bullet and Retraining

Robin's first career was as a travel agent. Back then just about everyone went to a travel agent to book their airfare, hotels, cruises, car rentals, and so forth. There was no Expedia or Travelocity or online airfare booking. Travel agents were the de facto experts in all things travel. It was an enjoyable career with great travel perks, but it never paid well. Robin's starting salary was $14,000 gross per year and it never went up much from there, despite the fact she became a highly competent travel agent with more than 12 years of experience in the business.

By the mid-1990s it had become painfully obvious that personal computers were making Robin's job obsolete. More and more people were booking their travel online, and who could blame them? It was fast, simple, and direct. Airlines and hotels began to realize they didn't need travel agents any more to represent their businesses. They no longer had to rely on a middleman: they could sell direct to their customers. As a result they started cutting commissions to travel agents.

Robin could see the writing on the wall. Being a travel agent simply was not a compatible career choice with wanting to retire early.

Reinventing Yourself

Robin realized she needed to invest in herself first before she could do much to help with investing for our retirement. By then it was 1998 and we had been saving for 7 years. That was nearly half of our 15-year plan, and yet we still only had a nest egg saved up of about $68,000.

We felt proud of that accomplishment on a personal level because we knew how hard it had been to set aside even that much money with salaries as low as ours had been. But clearly we were getting nowhere fast. I needed to rededicate myself to making more progress in my own field (I was a proposal coordinator making about $40,000 per year), and Robin needed to change fields altogether.

After much soul-searching she chose a career in nursing. She liked the idea of helping people and doing something meaningful, and, on the practical side, nursing paid reasonably well and there were openings all over the country for trained nurses. There was job security in the sense that no computer was going to make this career obsolete like it did her last.

So for 1½ years Robin went back to school again to reinvent herself and become a nurse. She passed her prerequisites at a local community college, got accepted to a rigorous one-year accelerated nursing program at Regis University in Denver, and ended up graduating third in her class. It helped that she was motivated and knew exactly what she wanted. She wasted no time getting hired as a nurse straight out of Regis and immediately put her newfound knowledge to the test starting in 2000.

The Cost of Retraining – and the Reward

The one-year nursing program set us back $20,000 (plus the lost opportunity cost of her being unemployed for 1½ years and not making the $15,000 per year she otherwise would have made). We had to borrow $10,500 in Stafford loans and another $5,000 from the bank to help cover the education costs.

Think of it: here we were, right in the midst of our primary investing years, and instead of earning money, Robin was needing to spend it on re-educating herself. But it was a necessary expense and we both knew it. She had to invest in herself first, and we trusted that in the long run it would be the right decision and bear fruit.

And it did. In her first year of nursing she more than doubled her previous salary. She went from making $15,000 as a travel agent to $39,000 as a nurse. Just six months after finishing her nursing program, we had already managed to pay back every cent of the loans.

By the following year she was making $45,000, and the year after that $50,000 and still going up. Now she was earning a salary that could genuinely help us with investing for early retirement.

Can you see how important it was for us to bite the bullet and pay for this training first? Even though it meant having to spend money over the short term, Robin earned enough in her first year of nursing to more than pay back her student loans. One-and-a-half years of retraining set her on a reliable earnings path for life.

Suddenly she was eminently employable. We could live anywhere in the country and know she could find work. And if we were to retire early and discover our finances were too tight, we knew in a pinch she could fall back on her nursing background and find temporary work to tide us over.

This gave us a newfound sense of confidence. We ended up being able to retire earlier than originally planned, in large part because we knew both our careers offered good opportunities for temporary employment should it ever become necessary. You may want to consider whether your own career skills are portable and can be carried into early retirement to make the transition a little less intimidating.

Earning Double

Imagine for a moment what it would be like to have a salary double what you're earning now. It's not impossible, especially if your current salary is under $30,000. Just picture it: if you were earning $50,000 or $60,000, then with a little self-discipline you could continue living at the same (or slightly higher) standard of living while investing the rest towards rapidly achieving financial independence.

Investing in yourself first will almost certainly be the best investment you ever make. Think of it this way: If you're earning $30,000 per year, it's going to take a lot of scrimping and saving to invest even $5,000 per year. But at $60,000 per year you could easily invest $20,000 and still have a sufficient amount left over to live on. That's *four times* the amount you could have invested otherwise. The stock market isn't going to give you those kinds of returns. But for as long as you stay employed, whether it be for 10 years or 20, you can count on similarly amazing results year after year. How many other investments can make that claim?

Retooling for a successful career is so important that we believe it is the one and only thing for which you should take out a loan even after you've begun saving for early retirement. Everywhere else in this book we recommend paying off your debts first, but if you find yourself in a low-paying or dead-end job, you simply have to remedy that situation first. Just be sure to choose a practical career path that will rapidly bear fruit afterwards.

Doing Your Career Homework

As an example of an impractical approach to career development, I offer up my own cautionary tale. I earned my master's degree in English literature in 1989. At the time I intended to become a college professor, which was a fine goal in and of itself. Fine except for the fact that I had never done a lick of teaching in my whole life and had no idea whether I would like it or not.

I knew I liked the perks of teaching and the prospect of working in an academic environment, but what about the job itself? If I had given any thought to how I would fit into the role, it might have saved me a lot of misdirected time and energy.

As it was, when I finally did get up in front of my first classroom, it took me all of five minutes to discover I wasn't at all suited to being a teacher. I wasn't comfortable standing in front of a large group of college freshmen and being the center of so much attention. How could it be that I was already partway down the road towards getting my Ph.D. before discovering this?

I somehow made it through that first semester of teaching, but I never grew more comfortable in the role. I could have saved myself and my poor students a whole lot of trouble if I had done the slightest bit of career homework first. My degree in English literature was not very useful outside the academic world, so it is with my own naive approach to career development in mind that I urge to do a little research first before going down a particular career path. First and foremost, make sure it's a job you can stomach doing!

Robin did her career homework before she became a nurse. Early on in the process she shadowed a nurse for a day, talked to other people who were LPNs and RNs, and learned from them which nursing programs were most highly respected. During her education she got plenty of hands-on experience in clinical settings, so she already knew what she was getting herself into by the time she got her degree.

Supercharging Your Career

Most of us live long enough these days to have more than one career – so go ahead, reinvent yourself. Pick a new career path and make it happen. The truth is, you need to *flourish* financially in order to build up a nest egg large enough to let you retire early. You can't just get by.

Once you make the switch to a better career, all things become possible. With Robin making $50,000 per year, we could live on her salary alone and invest all of my salary. Suddenly we could take giant strides forward. We did most of our really good investing after Robin's nursing career got underway – and that wasn't until more than halfway through our 15-year plan. At that point we were hitting on all cylinders and were able to sock away significant amounts of money in a relatively short period of time.

Imagine if Robin had begun her retraining at the beginning of our retirement planning. Instead of 7 years of higher wages, we might have had 14 years of solid earnings helping us along on our path to financial independence.

Investing in yourself first doesn't always mean going back to school for more education; it could mean simply applying yourself more vigorously to the job you already have. This was the case for me once I became a proposal coordinator. I already had the necessary education and skill set for my job, but what I needed was to apply myself with greater energy. I had to try harder, say yes more often, take on the harder projects no one else wanted to undertake, and work with increased efficiency and enthusiasm. I had to treat each proposal as if it mattered to me personally.

When I did that, the results spoke for themselves. We won more proposals, and over time I became more valuable to my company based on the skills I had developed. As I gained a better sense of my worth in the marketplace, I was able to parlay a job offer from a competing firm into an increased salary at my existing job. If you know you're doing meaningful work that adds to the company's bottom line, then being willing to ask respectfully for more compensation can be an important contributor to your career growth.

Our original retirement worksheets woefully underestimated just how much our salaries would grow – and how much extra money we would be able to invest as a result. We had to revise our yearly savings estimates significantly upwards in order to account for the new reality of two jobs paying solid wages. You may likewise find yourself pleasantly surprised on the upside. Do what you can to supercharge your career and you'll end up supercharging your investments as well.

Chapter 6.
Get Out of Debt

If you're not in debt, congratulations – you can skip this chapter! Otherwise we strongly recommend you get out of debt first before you start saving for retirement. Pay off credit card debts, car loans, college loans, and any other loans you might have so the only debt you have left is your home mortgage.

Why do we make an exception for home mortgages? Because buying a home is so expensive that most people find it impossible to own a home without first getting a long-term loan from a financial institution. Your home is also an investment over the long term, so there is good justification for owning rather than renting for so many years. But all other debt besides your home mortgage is manageable – and should be managed aggressively.

Your first priority should be to eliminate debt so you can start your investment program with a clean slate. Your second priority should be to build up a small reserve of cash to fall back on in case of emergency. Once those two priorities have been met, you're ready to begin investing in earnest for early retirement.

Why You Should Pay Down Debt Before Investing

You may be saying to yourself, "But I'm really anxious to start making some investments *now*! Why can't I pay down my debt and begin making investments at the same time?"

Well, in one specific instance you should. If you happen to have a 401(k) at work, we would recommend you invest the minimum amount necessary to take advantage of the full company match, which is essentially free money. But otherwise, unless free money is involved, it usually makes better sense to get out of debt first before beginning to invest. Here's why.

Let's say you get ambitious and manage to pay off your credit card balance with the 17% interest rate a whole year earlier than you would have otherwise. That's one whole year of *not* having to pay 17% interest – and that's the equivalent of getting a 17% guaranteed return on investment for the year. To put it another way, not having to pay 17% on a $1,000 balance on your credit card saves you $170, just as making 17% on a $1,000 investment makes you $170. Making $170 and saving $170 are two sides of the same coin.

Most people would agree 17% is a pretty good return on investment. We'd feel very pleased indeed if we could get that kind of return on a consistent basis. So it only makes financial sense to pay off the 17% credit card balance first, before beginning to invest elsewhere at what will probably be a lower rate of return. Even if you happen to have loans that only charge you 8% or 9% interest, that's still a pretty decent rate of *guaranteed* return. So pay them off first and be done with them.

Beyond the obvious financial rationale for paying off your debt early, there's also the psychological one. Simply put, it feels good to be out from under a load of debt and not owe anyone any money. It's like a burden has been lifted off your shoulders.

An emergency cash reserve lightens the load even more by giving you a financial cushion if your car should suddenly break down or your furnace should go on the fritz or some other big expense should hit unexpectedly. A small stash of cash is your get out of jail free card for when the unforeseen happens – which it inevitably will.

Why You Shouldn't Borrow From Yourself

As of January 2013, average credit card debt among households carrying such debt was a whopping $15,442. When you consider the average rate of interest on that debt is around 15%, it's no wonder we hear talk of people "drowning in debt" or being "up to their eyeballs in debt." Meanwhile, average student debt is nearly $35,000, so young people in particular are struggling to get out from under a mountain of debt that must often feel like it is crushing them.

If you are among the half of American households carrying an unpaid credit card balance over the past 12 months, your first order of business after landing a solid job should be to aggressively pay down that debt before it can become any more unmanageable.

Poor Future You

The sad truth is, each time you let the balance on your credit cards roll over another month, you're borrowing from your own future. You're essentially subsidizing "current you" by taking from "future you" and saying "put it on his tab." Let's be honest: future you isn't going to have any more money than current you has if you keep sticking him with the bill!

You pay in a big way when you borrow from your own future. You particularly pay in the form of exorbitant interest rates charged by credit card companies, which go out of their way to make it as easy as possible for you to pay the minimum balance each month and stay under water for another day, another month, another year. It's frankly in their own financial interest to keep you under water. They really don't mind seeing you drowning in debt (or at least struggling a little) because it means more money for them.

What a Deal: 19½ Years at Twice the Price

Here's a good rule to live by: never make just the minimum monthly payment on your credit cards. Here's why. Let's say you have $4,000 on a credit card with a 20% annual percentage rate on outstanding balances. And let's say you currently make the minimum payment of 3% per month. Now let's figure out together how much and how long it will take you to pay it back:

1. $4,000 (credit card balance) x 3% (minimum payment) = $120 minimum payment for the first month.

2. Out of that $120 minimum payment, $66.66 is interest ($4,000 x 20% annual interest rate ÷ 12 months = $66.66).

3. The remaining $53.34 is principal ($120 – $66.66 interest = $53.34 principal).

4. At the end of the first month, your remaining balance stands at $3,946.66 ($4,000 – $53.34 principal payment = $3,946.66).

5. The same calculation is performed next month, and the month after that, and so on, until the credit card debt is finally paid off. If you keep making just the minimum payments, your original credit card debt of $4,000 will cost you $8,741 to pay back. That's $4,000 to cover the original principal plus another $4,741 in interest – more than the original credit card debt itself!

6. It will take you 19½ years to make the 235 minimum payments!

Can you see how you end up sabotaging your own future when you play by the rules of the credit card companies? Stop playing by their rules and start playing by your own. Let's see what specific steps you can take to start getting out of debt right now.

Using Credit Card Calculators

Credit card calculators allow you to instantly calculate how long it will take you to get out of debt based on the monthly payment amount you enter. These free calculators are useful tools that let you experiment with different monthly scenarios. Paying even $50 more than the minimum monthly payment amount can make a huge difference, for example, in terms of the time it will take to pay off the balance and the total interest you'll pay. The more aggressive your payback plan, the more impressive the results.

We particularly like the tools offered at creditcards.com/calculators. Their Minimum Payment Calculator instantly shows you how painfully long and drawn-out the loan payment process is if you only make the minimum monthly payments. Their Payoff Calculator is even more helpful: it lets you run two useful scenarios. In the first, you enter the "Desired Months to Pay Off" your debt and the calculator automatically determines the monthly payment you would need to make to pay off your balance in the desired time. In the second scenario, you enter your "Desired Monthly Payment" amount and the calculator automatically determines the number of months it would take to pay off your balance. Calculators like this allow you to make informed choices about your future based on the specifics of your own situation.

Deciding Which Debts To Pay Off First

We recommend paying off the debt with the highest interest rate first, then moving on to the next-highest rate, and so on, in a logical progression until all your debts are paid off. Our thinking is, why give away any more of your money than you have to?

But another school of thought suggests you should get some quick wins under your belt by paying off the smallest debt first, enabling you to build up momentum to get your "debt snowball" rolling. This approach has some validity too. It's less logical financially but perhaps more agreeable psychologically.

Whichever approach works for you is fine, as long as you're making real progress towards reducing your overall debt.

Setting Monthly Goals to Tackle Debt

The best way to tackle debt is to set monthly goals for yourself. Setting goals gives you a game plan and lets you know what you're aiming for. It's important to be as realistic as possible when making your plan. If you set the bar too high, you're setting yourself up for failure. If you set it too low, it will take you too long to reach your goal, and that can be discouraging in its own right. You want to find a balance point between time and money that feels right to you.

Let's look at an example. Let's say you have $20,000 in debt. That includes all your debt – credit cards, the last few payments on a car loan, and a college loan. You want to pay it off as quickly as possible, so you go to one of the debt payment calculators online to determine what is feasible.

First you try plugging in 12 months as your desired payoff date. The results say it would take nearly $1,800 per month to pay off the debt in that period of time, and you realize straight away there's no way you can afford that kind of monthly payment given what you're currently earning. Next you try 24 months and 36 months, and the results come in at around $950 and $700 per month respectively, both of which seem feasible. Last, you try 48 months and discover that would run you $550 per month, which isn't *that* much less than paying it off in 36 months. For an extra $150 per month you could be done in three years instead of four. Plus, something inside you just groans at the thought of still being in debt four years from now, so you decide to eliminate that option.

Now you've bracketed your solution. You know you *can't* pay it off in 12 months and you know you *don't want to* wait four years to pay it off if you can help it. That leaves you with two solutions in the middle: either 24 months or 36 months.

Which of the options you choose is up to you. If you want to get out of debt more than anything else in the world, go with the two-year plan. If you want to live a little more comfortably in the coming years, go with the three-year plan. Either way, you've made a good plan. You've come up with a way to pay off your debts in two or three years' time, which feels about right. It hits that balance point between time and money.

With either of these plans, you can make adjustments as you go. If you choose the 36-month option but your salary jumps significantly the following year, you can always increase your monthly payments. Or if you choose the 24-month option but unanticipated expenses crop up, you can always decrease your payments to bring them in line with the 36-month plan.

The good news is, the self-discipline it takes to set monthly goals and get out of debt is exactly the same discipline needed to save large amounts of money for early retirement. Think of getting out of debt as a trial run. Once you've done that, you're ready for the main event: saving up enough money to become financially independent for life.

Using One Primary Credit Card

We recommend you use just one primary credit card and pay off the balance in full each month. Don't shortchange your own future by living in debt for even one month if you can help it.

Having a single card you actively use makes it easy to track exactly how much you owe each month so there are no unpleasant surprises. We believe keeping things simple and knowing where you stand each month trumps the small savings you might realize by using a slew of different credit cards, each specific to one store. Your wallet and your financial burdens will be lighter with just the one credit card.

Once you're certain you have the self-discipline it takes to use only one card, you may want to consider having a backup credit card stored somewhere safe just in case your main card is lost or stolen or otherwise becomes inactive. More than once now, we've had our primary card stop working due to a potential security breach at some store or other. Although a new card was automatically reissued and mailed to our home address, we were overseas at the time and couldn't pick it up. In such circumstances a backup credit card can be a real life saver.

Chapter 7.
Start Saving Early

We sometimes wish we could have a do-over of our twenties from a personal finances standpoint. Instead of making focused decisions that could have allowed us to start saving for financial independence sooner, we drifted sideways and didn't start saving in earnest until age 31. If we had stepped into good-paying jobs immediately out of college, who knows how early we might have retired?

We certainly encourage younger readers to be more practical than we were in terms of your educational and career choices, because if you *do* make the right decisions early on, you could be financially independent by age 35 or 40. Alternatively, you could choose to keep working five or ten years longer and let the power of compounding *really* work its magic for you, giving you a substantially larger nest egg.

The Power of Compounding

The earlier you can start saving for retirement the better, since it gives your investments more time to compound. Compounding, simply put, is earning interest on your interest. When interest is added to your principal, from that point forward it too earns interest. Compounding is at the very heart of a get rich slowly approach to investing.

Suppose you put $10,000 in a bank certificate of deposit that pays 5% interest annually. At the end of one year your balance will have grown by $500 (5% of your initial $10,000) to $10,500. Assuming you leave the entire amount in the CD, your principal the next year will stand at $10,500 + 5% = $11,025. Over the course of 25 years, here's how your initial investment will grow:

Years	Total (5% Growth)
0 years	$10,000
5 years	$12,763
10 years	$16,289
15 years	$20,789
20 years	$26,533
25 years	$33,864

That's the power of compounding for you. Simply by "doing nothing" and leaving your investment in place to grow, you can watch your initial investment double and double again. Your money starts to make money for you, which in turn makes your road to retirement that much easier as the years pass.

Time is your friend when it comes to investing. That's why the earlier you can get started the better. If you were to start investing at age 25, you could retire at age 50 and still have a 25-year investment time horizon, giving your money plenty of time to grow. Compounding is powerful enough that it can take an average investor and make him into a great one simply by virtue of his having started investing at a young enough age.

Did you know compound interest was once regarded as the worst form of usury and was severely condemned by Roman law? Times certainly have changed: now gladiatorial combat is out and compounding is in. Since compounding is fully legal now, we suggest you take full advantage of it as you save for retirement.

The effects of compounding become even more evident if your investment earns a higher annual rate of return. In the example above we assume a 5% annual return. But let's say you put the same $10,000 into a mutual fund earning, on average, 10% per year. Here's how your investment would grow:

Years	Total (10% Growth)
0 years	$10,000
5 years	$16,105
10 years	$25,937
15 years	$41,772
20 years	$67,275
25 years	$108,347

By accepting more risk and investing in a stock mutual fund instead of a bank CD, our hypothetical investor has earned a much greater return. Notice how the effects of compounding become more pronounced in later years. For instance, the balance jumps from around $67,000 at the 20-year mark to $108,000 at the 25-year mark. That's $41,000 earned in just five years. This remarkable growth stems from the fact that the capital base is much larger to begin with at the 20-year mark, so a 10% average return over the next five years has a much greater effect.

This goes to show why a long investment time horizon is so important. The longer you wait to tap your money, the more dramatic the returns can become in later years. (Assuming, of course, that the markets cooperate on your behalf, which isn't always the case.)

As a final comparison, let's say that instead of letting the money compound, you simply take the 10% earnings out each year and use it for cash. That's $1,000 per year in your pocket, but at quite the price. Here's how the two scenarios measure up:

	Take the Cash	**Let It Compound**
Initial investment:	$10,000	$10,000
Earnings in 25 years' time:	$25,000	$98,347
Total:	$35,000	$108,347

That's a difference of over $73,000 between the two scenarios. Enough said!

Using Investing Calculators

Online investing calculators make it easy to see how your monthly contributions compound over time, helping you to get rich slowly. One of our favorites is at daveramsey.com (under the "Tools" tab). You plug in your 1) starting balance (if any), 2) estimated annual rate of return, 3) monthly contribution, 4) number of years you plan to contribute, and 5) total number of years you'll be allowing the money to compound, then hit the "Calculate" key and up pops a bar chart showing you the results.

The chart is intuitively easy to understand. For each scenario you run, it instantly shows you the total contributions made by you versus the total amount earned as a result of compounding. It also shows the year in which you cross the $1 million mark. It's a great tool and free to use.

Try plugging in different values to experiment with different scenarios until you hit upon a scenario that feels right to you. A good scenario is one that balances the needs of today with the needs of tomorrow. You don't want to drive yourself crazy by setting the monthly investment bar too high. Also, keep in mind that any scenario is just that: a reasonable guess about the future that may not match up all that closely with reality. But that's okay, plans can be adjusted. The important thing is to *have* a plan.

How Compounding Can Help Parents in Particular

The magic of compounding is especially important for parents wondering how they can ever manage to save up enough for early retirement. By adding five or ten years to their overall investment plan, parents can still reach their financial goals while providing for their children's needs at the same time. They can do right by their kids and by themselves by methodically investing smaller sums of money but doing it over a longer period of time. It may take them a few extra years, but the result is still a nice, tidy nest egg – and at an age young enough to enjoy it. Take a look at these two scenarios to see what we mean:

Scenario #1.
Couple with no kids saves **$3,000** per mo. for **15** years with a 9% annual return to accumulate a $1.1 million nest egg

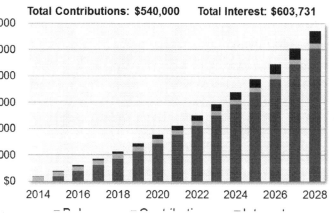

15-Year Value: $1,143,731

Total Contributions: $540,000   Total Interest: $603,731

Scenario #2.
Couple with kids saves **$1,000** per mo. for **25** years with a 9% annual return to accumulate a $1.1 million nest egg

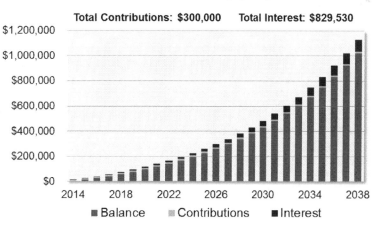

25-Year Value: $1,129,530

Total Contributions: $300,000   Total Interest: $829,530

■ Balance ▪ Contributions ■ Interest

In each case the end result is roughly the same, and quite impressive: a nest egg of over $1.1 million (not including home equity). The couple with no kids has invested $3,000 per month for 15 years to reach their goal. The parents have invested smaller amounts but over a longer period of time – $1,000 per month for 25 years – to reach their goal.

Take a moment to compare the total contributions and total interest in the two scenarios and note the huge variation between them. The couple with no kids has invested $540,000 of their own money and earned $604,000 as a result of compounding. Not bad. But the parents have invested $300,000 of their own money and earned nearly $830,000 as a result of compounding! They have had to put in a lot less effort to achieve a similar result, thanks to the power of compounding over time.

If these folks had all started investing at age 30, the couple with no kids would be 45 when they retired and the parents would be 55. Compounding helps in both cases, but it is especially important for the parents who have wisely given themselves a longer time horizon in which to invest.

Riding the Compounding Tailwind to Retirement

We believe the hardest years of investing by far are the earliest ones because you're getting so little tailwind in terms of compounding. It feels like you're going nowhere fast. For us it seemed to take forever to reach that first $100,000 mark.

Then things got easier. The $100,000 already saved up started working *for* us, compounding, giving us that all-important tailwind we had been missing before. It didn't take nearly as long or seem nearly so arduous to get from $100,000 to $200,000, and this trend continued into the future.

So beginning investors, take heart: it really does get easier as the years go by. You can thank the power of compounding for that. If you hang tough and keep investing as much as you can in those early years, your perseverance will pay off in the end. It helps to remember that the money you save early on is the money that will compound the most over the years.

Chapter 8.
Determine Your Retirement Income Needs

Figuring out how much money you're likely to need on an annual basis in the somewhat distant future is no easy matter. But you can start with this simple premise: your expenses will almost certainly be lower then than they are now.

Why? Well, for starters, you won't be needing to invest for retirement any more once you're retired, obviously, so those "expenses" will go away. In addition, you won't be making mortgage payments any more, and any expenses associated with raising children and sending them off to college will no longer apply. Certain work-related expenses will drop away once you no longer need to make the daily commute. Significant home and yard improvements should be a thing of the past. And your taxes will almost certainly go down compared to what you're paying now.

On the other hand, your health care costs may increase somewhat, as well as your travel and leisure expenses. Then there's inflation, which continually eats away at the value of your dollar year after year. Inflation adds a whole new dimension to the discussion.

We'll talk about each of these factors in a moment, but first we'd like to discuss the strong differences of opinion that exist about how best to determine your future yearly income needs.

Two Methods for Calculating Future Income

One approach touted by many financial and insurance firms is to start with your *current income* then multiply that income by 70% or 80% to determine the amount you're likely to need in the future. We think this method is fundamentally flawed. It tends to result in an overestimate that makes people think they need to save a bigger nest egg than they really do. It goes without saying this benefits the same financial firms that recommend it, since it means more money flowing into their coffers.

Because salaries tend to be at their highest towards the end of a person's career, a catch-22 situation can result in which ever higher salaries lead to ever higher estimates of future needs, which in turn drives the perceived need for an ever bigger nest egg. All of this leads to the belief that you need to keep on working, keep on saving, keep on striving. But the truth is, current income has little to do with how much you'll need once you retire. Let's use our own example as a case in point.

Towards the end of our working years we were making the most we had ever earned, as tends to be the case. Firms recommending the income approach to calculating your retirement needs typically suggest you take the average of your final ten years of annual income. They tell you to multiply that amount by 70% and 80% to get a range representing the low end and high end of what you're likely to need in order to maintain your current standard of living in retirement.

Applying this formula to our own situation, our average annual income over the ten-year period prior to retirement was $106,885. Multiplying this amount by 70% and 80% gives you a range of $74,820 to $85,508, with the median point of the range being $80,164.

But in actual fact we have lived quite comfortably on $40,000 per year each year since retiring. Our standard of living has remained virtually the same as before except that it includes a lot more travel. You can see from this example just how flawed the 70-80 approach can be. Any method that misses the mark by more than double should be considered suspect.

If you are aggressively saving for early retirement, then the results of the 70-80 method tend to be particularly skewed. A large chunk of your income is going towards investments and is thus off the table in terms of what you're actually living on at present. Our investments, for instance, often amounted to over 40% of our income during the latter years of our employment. Our taxes were also at their highest during this period. Thus anyone pushing hard to retire early is likely to be led astray by using current income as the means for determining how much they'll need once they retire.

Instead we recommend you start with *current expenses* to determine your retirement needs. Actual living expenses in the present day give you a better take on what you'll need down the road, once you have subtracted out the ones that no longer apply and have made appropriate adjustments for inflation.

It's particularly important to get the yearly retirement income number right since it feeds directly into the calculation of how big your nest egg needs to be. The difference between being able to live on $40,000 per year and $80,000 per year is the difference between needing to save up a nest egg of $1 million and $2 million. Think of how many extra years of work it would take to amass an extra million dollars in savings. Thus the yearly retirement income estimate becomes magnified in terms of its potential impact on your life and the decisions you make about your own future.

Making an Initial Estimate Based on Current Expenses

Let's begin by taking a look at your current living expenses. Let's say you and your spouse currently have a combined gross income of $100,000, or $75,000 net after taxes. Now, using broad brushstrokes, let's eliminate a few of the major expenses you probably won't have once you retire.

For starters, the mortgage will be paid off by the time you retire, so that's, say, $1,250 per month or $15,000 per year you won't have to worry about. Perhaps you've also been putting away $3,000 per year for your kids' college education. And let's say you've identified another $1,000 per year in additional expenses related to kids, jobs, home renovation, yard maintenance, and so forth that you feel fairly certain will no longer apply once you're retired.

Finally, let's say you're in your primary investing years and have been socking away $20,000 per year into your retirement funds. Of course, that "expense" will no longer be there once you're retired. So:

$100,000 (combined gross income)
-$25,000 (taxes at 25%)
-$15,000 (mortgage payments)
-$3,000 (kids' college fund)
-$1,000 (misc. expenses related to kids, jobs, home improvements, etc.)
-$20,000 (retirement investments)
$36,000 (adjusted net income)

This hypothetical scenario suggests you and your spouse could be getting by on as little as $36,000 net per year if it weren't for mortgage payments, extra expenses associated with kids and job, and the need to save for college and retirement. That's some pretty frugal living you're doing when you consider it that way.

But now the pendulum has to swing the other way. You've done some subtraction, now you need to do some addition. To make an accurate assessment of how much you'll need once you retire, you have to add money back in to account for inflation, taxes, and potentially higher health care costs in retirement. (We won't try to account for increased travel expenses in this example because they can vary so much from one person to the next, but you may want to pad your estimate slightly higher if you expect to travel intensively once retired. See Chapter 17, "Extended Travel in Retirement," for a discussion of affordable long-term travel.)

Adjusting for Inflation

Inflation on a nationwide basis rises by an average of roughly 3% per year according to the Consumer Price Index, which measures the cost of a basket of common goods and services Americans buy (food, clothing, housing, medical care, energy, etc.). The CPI is a national average of prices, but based on our own experience we think 3% is a bit high for calculating your personal inflation rate. If you live consciously, you can keep inflation from having as strong of an impact on your life as it might have on the economy as a whole.

For instance, the price of seeing a movie in a theater may have gone up to $12 per ticket, but that doesn't mean you can't make the conscious decision to wait and see the same movie at home for a dollar. And just because a restaurant raises its lunch price to $20 doesn't mean you can't make the conscious decision to eat somewhere else more affordably. You might do takeout for half the price or make lunch at home for even less. So while we can't ignore the effects of inflation, we can mitigate its effects to some degree by making intelligent decisions in our personal lives.

We think a personal inflation rate of 2% is closer to the mark than 3%, and that's the number we'll use here. But keep in mind high inflation can rear its ugly head at any time and pose a serious problem for retirees on a fixed income. Keep an eye on what's happening in the real world and adjust your calculations and thought processes accordingly.

Based on a personal inflation rate of 2%, to have the equivalent of $36,000 in today's dollars you'd need $36,000 + 2% = $36,720 next year. The year after that you'd need $36,720 + 2% = $37,454, and so on. In 15 years' time, to have the buying power $36,000 gives you today, you'd need $48,451. For simplicity's sake let's round the number up to $49,000.

Adjusting for Taxes in Retirement

The *net* amount our hypothetical couple will need in retirement is $49,000. However, when they withdraw money from their retirement accounts they'll typically be withdrawing gross proceeds and may need to pay some amount of income tax on that amount. Let's assume 10% taxes, which may sound low, but in actual fact we've had several years go by since retiring in which we've owed zero dollars in taxes (see "Income Taxes in Retirement" in Chapter 3 for details).

For now let's assume 10% income taxes and add $5,444 to the $49,000 to arrive at a gross income of $54,444. (In case you're interested in doing the math, divide the net amount of $49,000 by 90% to arrive at the gross amount.) For simplicity's sake we'll round the number up to $55,000.

Adjusting for Health Care in Retirement

You may also want to add some money in for potentially higher health care costs in retirement. As of 2014, the Affordable Care Act will make health care much more affordable for early retirees on a budget, as we discuss in Chapter 16 ("Health Care in Retirement"). The effects of this new legislation are significant enough that we're only going to add $1,000 to our hypothetical couple's total, and that's mostly to account for higher out-of-pocket expenses associated with things like dental and vision care that aren't necessarily covered under the new law.

Keep in mind you're probably not paying zero dollars for health care currently. Even if your employer covers you, you're almost certainly paying something into the system. According to the *Employer Health Benefits 2011 Survey* by the Kaiser Family Foundation, for example, workers with family coverage contribute, on average, $344 per month ($4,129 annually) towards their health insurance premiums. The $1,000 we're adding is on top of whatever amount our hypothetical couple is already paying for health and dental care during their working years.

If, after reading Chapter 16, you still expect your health care costs in early retirement to be significantly higher, you can use whatever number you feel most accurately reflects your future reality.

Calculation Summary

Our couple's estimated annual retirement expenses now stand at $56,000. This estimate of their future income needs is grounded in the reality of their current situation while also having been appropriately adjusted for inflation. While it may not be exact, it lets us proceed with a reasonable degree of confidence.

Since we've provided a lot of detailed information here involving a fair amount of math, let's take a moment to sum up:

1. Start with your current gross annual income $100,000
2. Subtract out annual federal and state taxes -$25,000
3. Subtract out annual mortgage payments, kids' college fund expenses, home and job expenses, etc. that no longer apply -$19,000
4. Subtract out annual retirement investments <u>-$20,000</u>

$36,000

5. Add 2% per year (e.g., for 15 years) to account for inflation ($36,000 + 2%, $36,720 + 2%, etc.) +$13,000
6. Account for 10% income taxes in retirement ($49,000 ÷ 90% = $54,444 - $49,000 = $5,444, rounded up to $6,000) +$6,000
7. Add $1,000 per year (or an amount you feel is appropriate to your situation) to account for higher health care costs in early retirement <u>+$1,000</u>

$56,000

Now all that remains is to calculate the size of the nest egg itself – which is the subject of the next chapter. We think you'll be glad to discover there's very little math involved in doing that.

Chapter 9.
Calculate Your Nest Egg

Perhaps the thought has occurred to you, What exactly constitutes my nest egg? Is the equity in my home a part of it? And what about the money in my 401(k) and IRA that I don't plan on touching until after I'm 59½? Does that count towards my nest egg when I'm trying to determine how much is safe to withdraw in the initial years of my early retirement?

These are fair questions and ones we pondered ourselves as we were nearing early retirement. We'll do our best to provide some guidance based on our own thinking about these issues both before and after retiring.

What Constitutes Your Nest Egg?

Your nest egg should consist only of liquid assets such as stocks, bonds, and cash, not illiquid assets such as real estate. Real estate is harder to sell and more cumbersome to work with if you want to generate cash for current living expenses. That said, if you plan on downsizing your home once you retire, whatever amount you *won't* be needing for home-buying purposes in the future can be turned into liquid assets that do count towards your nest egg.

How Much of Your Home Counts?

Prior to retirement we included all of the equity in our home as part of our nest egg calculation since we didn't plan on owning a home once we retired. And indeed we did sell our home after retiring and lived for two years as nomads by choice, renting wherever our travels happened to take us. For those two years our assets were all liquid.

But we came to miss having a home base, so we ended up purchasing a small condo, which meant taking $100,000 off the table in terms of liquid assets and putting it back into illiquid real estate. In effect this amount no longer counted towards our retirement nest egg because it no longer generated funds we could use to live on (short of renting it out for periods of time, which we have considered doing but haven't done so far). The condo still counts towards our net assets but not towards our nest egg.

In retrospect it would have been wiser for us to factor in the need for a downsized home in retirement as opposed to no home at all. By subtracting $100,000 out of our total holdings, we could have more accurately assessed the real size of our nest egg as we were planning for retirement.

For this reason we recommend you set aside a portion of your home's equity (say, between one quarter and one half) for future real estate purposes. This amount can be applied either to a downsized home or to covering rental costs wherever you may happen to live in the world if you choose not to own a home for a period of time. Either way, you're ahead of the game if you don't have to subtract this amount out of your nest egg once you retire.

Are Your 401(k) and Roth IRA Assets Part of Your Nest Egg?

Deciding whether 401(k) and Roth IRA assets are liquid or illiquid in the years before you can access them without penalty is admittedly something of a gray area. Here are our thoughts on the matter, although others might reasonably disagree.

We recommend you do include 401(k) and Roth IRA amounts when calculating your nest egg, even if you plan on relying solely on the money in your taxable account in the years prior to turning 59½. The stock, bond, and mutual fund assets in these accounts really are liquid and could be sold for cash quickly if need be. Of course your intention is to leave them untouched for years to come since you would otherwise have to pay a penalty tax for accessing them prematurely, but they are nevertheless still liquid in nature.

Just because you choose (wisely) to rely solely on the taxable portion of your liquid assets during your early retirement years doesn't mean the other tax-advantaged liquid assets don't exist. They do exist and in fact are likely to grow in the years to come, providing you with a steady stream of income when the time is right. Not factoring them into your nest egg would be to ignore a significant and ever-increasing portion of your portfolio.

Using the 4% Rule to Calculate Your Nest Egg

Once you've determined your annual retirement income needs, as we did in Chapter 8, the next step is easy. You can use what's known as the 4% rule to estimate the nest egg you'll need in order to safely generate that amount. Let's start with $56,000, the annual retirement income amount from our example in the previous chapter. Using a variation of the 4% rule called the "Rule of 25," you can perform a quick back-of-the-napkin nest egg calculation. Simply multiply the income amount by 25 to determine the size of the nest egg you'll need. For example:

$56,000 (annual retirement income) x 25 = $1.4 million nest egg

It's as straightforward as that. A nest egg of $1.4 million will generate an annual retirement income of $56,000 for our hypothetical couple. Note that dividing the income amount by 4% will get you the same result as multiplying by 25. The two approaches are mathematically the same in terms of providing you with an answer as to the size of the nest egg you need.

Perhaps an easier way to visualize how the 4% rule works is to start with the nest egg amount itself and multiply by 4% to determine the yearly income amount it will safely generate, as follows:

$500,000 nest egg x 4% = $20,000 income per year
$750,000 nest egg x 4% = $30,000 income per year
$1,000,000 nest egg x 4% = $40,000 income per year
$1,250,000 nest egg x 4% = $50,000 income per year
$1,500,000 nest egg x 4% = $60,000 income per year
$1,750,000 nest egg x 4% = $70,000 income per year
$2,000,000 nest egg x 4% = $80,000 income per year

Don't be surprised if the nest egg amount you calculate is larger than you were anticipating. Inflation can have that effect. But keep in mind your salary will also be keeping up with – and hopefully outpacing – inflation over the coming 15 to 20 years, so what may seem like an impossibly large number now should feel more attainable as the years pass and your salary increases. Compounding will also assist you in reaching your goal, giving you a tailwind in the later years of your plan.

Why Is 4% a Safe Withdrawal Amount?

You may be wondering, Why 4%? Why not more or less than that? Doesn't 4% seem artificially low? Couldn't you take out, say, 6% and still be okay? And how safe is safe when people tell you 4% is a safe amount to withdraw? Let's try to answer a few of these questions.

The Original 4% Rule

Most financial planners these days agree on some variation of the 4% rule. As originally formulated by William Bengen, a certified financial planner in the early 1990s, the rule states you can safely withdraw 4% of your nest egg in your first year of retirement and increase that amount annually thereafter for inflation without too much risk of depleting your nest egg over 30 years.

Let's say you have a $1 million nest egg. According to the traditional application of the 4% rule, your first year of retirement you could take out $1 million x 4% =

$40,000. Next year, adjusting for inflation (let's say it's at 2%), you could take out $40,000 + 2% = $40,800. The year after that, if inflation were at 3%, you could take out $40,800 + 3% = $42,024, and so on. That's the 4% rule at its most basic.

Economists have done careful historical modeling and run extensive algorithms (called Monte Carlo simulations) to arrive at the conclusion that 4% is a reasonably safe amount to withdraw from your portfolio each year. Bengen himself concluded that drawing down just 1% more than that per year – that is, 5% plus inflation adjustments – resulted in a 30% chance of a retiree's nest egg being depleted too soon. For the average retiree that is simply too high a risk.

At or Near the Limit of Safety

When we were originally planning for early retirement, it seemed to us the 4% rule was overly conservative. We wondered why we couldn't safely withdraw 6% or more per year if our investments were earning, say, 9%. But we've come to realize that prolonged downturns in the market can wreak havoc with an investment portfolio, especially in the early years of one's retirement, and any good rule of thumb has to account for that possibility. A few years of negative returns, combined with higher than normal withdrawals, could deplete a portfolio to the point where it can no longer sustain itself but instead begins a slow spiral towards zero.

While the stock market may return an *average* of 9% over the long term, it can be all over the map in the short term, and the 4% rule is designed to compensate for that. It's also helpful to remember that posted annual returns are typically pre-tax and do not account for inflation. A 9% return is closer to a 7% real return after factoring in inflation, and it's even lower than that after factoring in taxes. When all of these issues are taken into consideration, 4% turns out to be the percentage that is at or near the limit of safety. Nearly all economic models agree that your nest egg is at serious risk of being depleted too soon if you are consistently withdrawing 6% or more, so keep your withdrawals in the 4% to 5% range if you want to stand a reasonable chance of seeing your portfolio last longer than you do.

Unfortunately there is no such thing as ironclad safety when it comes to investing, only relative safety. Under terrible economic conditions it would be possible to deplete your portfolio even if you only took out 4% per year. But the best you can do is err on the conservative side so the odds are in your favor and recognize there are no guarantees either in life or in investing.

Modifying the 4% Rule to Address Limitations

Of course the 4% rule is only a rule of thumb and not an exact science, but it serves as a good financial yardstick for determining the approximate size of the nest egg you'll need. We think it works best when, like any rule of thumb, it is applied with a strong dose of common sense. The rule as originally formulated has some important limitations, so we recommend you use it but in a modified fashion as described below.

Is Thirty Years Enough?

The chief problem with the 4% rule as originally articulated is that it was only meant to apply to 30 years' worth of retirement living. But with people living longer and retiring earlier, this assumption no longer holds true in every case. You might need to fund 40 or even 50 years' worth of retirement living.

Our solution to this problem is to effectively turn off the automatic inflation adjustment feature built into the original rule. If you do not adjust for inflation every year or make only minimal tweaks – especially in the early years of your retirement – then you are hedging your bets in favor of a healthy investment portfolio that is likely to outlast you.

Inflation has been so low over the past few years that we have been able to go six years so far without needing to adjust our annual withdrawal amounts. Only now are we beginning to notice a real difference in our buying power. By minimizing inflation adjustments, we give our portfolio a better chance of not only sustaining itself but growing over the long term. This increases the odds it will be there to support us 40 or even 50 years down the line if necessary.

As for inflation in our later years, we feel we can rely on future social security payments to help with that. In fact that is exactly how we think of social security: as a hedge against inflation in the distant future. We aren't expecting much more from it than that, especially since our payments will be reduced from the norm since we retired so early. (Social security payments are calculated based on your 35 highest-earning working years; if you work less years than that, you'll have some years with zero income averaged in – which will lower your payout.)

Tweaking Withdrawals Based on Actual Conditions

Another problem with the 4% rule as traditionally formulated is that it makes no attempt to account for changes in spending behavior due to big-picture changes in the economy. The rule is applied blindly, in essence. Whether you are in the depths of a recession or at the heights of a roaring bull market, it always recommends you withdraw exactly the same amount per year (other than compensating for inflation). This makes it simple to apply but inflexible when it comes to rolling with the punches that the financial markets sometimes throw at you.

In response to this concern, many economists advocate starting with the 4% rule but tweaking your withdrawals from year to year based on actual market conditions. This makes perfect sense to us. If the stock market is performing splendidly year after year, then you shouldn't feel obliged to artificially limit yourself to 4% plus the inflation rate. In such a situation you might be warranted in taking out 6% of your nest egg (or more) in a given year – as long as it doesn't become your new norm. After a particularly good string of years, you might splurge on that around-the-world trip you've always dreamed of before returning to a more normal withdrawal rate the following year.

On the other hand, if the economy is in a deep and prolonged recession, then blindly applying the 4% rule – which traditionally would call for you to *increase* your withdrawal amounts in order to account for inflation – would be questionable at best. You might end up materially weakening the health of your portfolio and decreasing its chances of survival over the long term. Under such conditions it would be wise to withdraw less than 4% (or at least not adjust for inflation) in order to protect your portfolio from further erosion. Increasing the flexibility of the 4% rule in such a fashion offers a more pragmatic, eyes-wide-open approach to drawing down your nest egg.

Achieving a Self-Sustaining Portfolio

A self-sustaining portfolio is your overall financial goal once you retire. A portfolio that is growing at a slow pace is a portfolio capable of keeping up with inflation and providing you with a slightly higher annual income as the years pass. Modifying the 4% rule by 1) turning off automatic inflation adjustments in favor of manual adjustments, and 2) tweaking your withdrawal rates based on actual market conditions should allow you to achieve this goal.

Using Retirement Calculators

You can use online retirement calculators in conjunction with the 4% rule to determine the approximate size of the nest egg you'll need. In Chapter 7 we mentioned one we particularly like at daveramsey.com (under the "Tools" tab). It creates a bar chart showing how your money compounds from year to year and lets you plug in different values to experiment with different scenarios.

Another nifty online tool is the Retirement Nest Egg Calculator on Vanguard's website. (Just type "Vanguard nest egg calculator" into Google and it will provide you with the link, which is rather long and cumbersome). The calculator runs 5,000 independent Monte Carlo simulations with just the click of a button.

Sliding bars lets you specify four data points: 1) how many years your portfolio needs to last, 2) your current portfolio balance, 3) how much you expect to spend from your portfolio each year, and 4) the percentage of stocks, bonds, and cash in your portfolio. Based on this information it calculates the probability of your portfolio lasting the number of years you've specified. If you're not satisfied with the results, you can tweak the sliding bars to explore different what-if scenarios.

Chapter 10.
Make a Long-Term Investment Plan

When making a long-term investment plan it helps to be able to clearly state your goal so there is no confusion about where you are heading. For example: "I want to retire in 15 years and have a nest egg of $1.5 million in order to generate $60,000 in income annually." To be able to put together a goal statement like this you need to work backwards, in essence, and complete three steps, two of which you've already completed in the previous two chapters:

1) Estimate your yearly income needs once you retire.
2) Calculate your nest egg based on these yearly income needs.
3) Put together a detailed plan outlining how many years it will take to save up your nest egg and how much you'll need to invest each year.

This chapter tackles the all-important third step. You may already have an initial sense of the number of years until your target retirement date, but completing this step will help you refine that understanding. By the end of it you'll have a much better grasp on how much you'll need to invest each year in order to accomplish your goal in the desired number of years.

Exercise #1: Investing the Same Amount Each Year

Let's get started by taking a look at the chart on the following page, which shows the results of steadily investing $15,000, $20,000, $25,000, and $30,000 per year for 15 years and 20 years assuming a consistent 9% annual return.

$15,000 Per Year

Year	Amount Invested	Plus Prev. Year's Total	Plus 9% Return	Grand Total
2014	$15,000	$0	$1,350	$16,350
2015	$15,000	$31,350	$2,822	$34,172
2016	$15,000	$49,172	$4,425	$53,597
2017	$15,000	$68,597	$6,174	$74,771
2018	$15,000	$89,771	$8,079	$97,850
2019	$15,000	$112,850	$10,157	$123,007
2020	$15,000	$138,007	$12,421	$150,427
2021	$15,000	$165,427	$14,888	$180,316
2022	$15,000	$195,316	$17,578	$212,894
2023	$15,000	$227,894	$20,510	$248,404
2024	$15,000	$263,404	$23,706	$287,111
2025	$15,000	$302,111	$27,190	$329,301
2026	$15,000	$344,301	$30,987	$375,288
2027	$15,000	$390,288	$35,126	$425,414
2028	$15,000	$440,414	$39,637	**$480,051**
2029	$15,000	$495,051	$44,555	$539,606
2030	$15,000	$554,606	$49,915	$604,520
2031	$15,000	$619,520	$55,757	$675,277
2032	$15,000	$690,277	$62,125	$752,402
2033	$15,000	$767,402	$69,066	**$836,468**

$20,000 Per Year

Year	Amount Invested	Plus Prev. Year's Total	Plus 9% Return	Grand Total
2014	$20,000	$0	$1,800	$21,800
2015	$20,000	$41,800	$3,762	$45,562
2016	$20,000	$65,562	$5,901	$71,463
2017	$20,000	$91,463	$8,232	$99,694
2018	$20,000	$119,694	$10,772	$130,467
2019	$20,000	$150,467	$13,542	$164,009
2020	$20,000	$184,009	$16,561	$200,569
2021	$20,000	$220,569	$19,851	$240,421
2022	$20,000	$260,421	$23,438	$283,859
2023	$20,000	$303,859	$27,347	$331,206
2024	$20,000	$351,206	$31,609	$382,814
2025	$20,000	$402,814	$36,253	$439,068
2026	$20,000	$459,068	$41,316	$500,384
2027	$20,000	$520,384	$46,835	$567,218
2028	$20,000	$587,218	$52,850	**$640,068**
2029	$20,000	$660,068	$59,406	$719,474
2030	$20,000	$739,474	$66,553	$806,027
2031	$20,000	$826,027	$74,342	$900,369
2032	$20,000	$920,369	$82,833	$1,003,202
2033	$20,000	$1,023,202	$92,088	**$1,115,291**

$25,000 Per Year

Year	Amount Invested	Plus Prev. Year's Total	Plus 9% Return	Grand Total
2014	$25,000	$0	$2,250	$27,250
2015	$25,000	$52,250	$4,703	$56,953
2016	$25,000	$81,953	$7,376	$89,328
2017	$25,000	$114,328	$10,290	$124,618
2018	$25,000	$149,618	$13,466	$163,083
2019	$25,000	$188,083	$16,928	$205,011
2020	$25,000	$230,011	$20,701	$250,712
2021	$25,000	$275,712	$24,814	$300,526
2022	$25,000	$325,526	$29,297	$354,823
2023	$25,000	$379,823	$34,184	$414,007
2024	$25,000	$439,007	$39,511	$478,518
2025	$25,000	$503,518	$45,317	$548,835
2026	$25,000	$573,835	$51,645	$625,480
2027	$25,000	$650,480	$58,543	$709,023
2028	$25,000	$734,023	$66,062	**$800,085**
2029	$25,000	$825,085	$74,258	$899,343
2030	$25,000	$924,343	$83,191	$1,007,533
2031	$25,000	$1,032,533	$92,928	$1,125,461
2032	$25,000	$1,150,461	$103,542	$1,254,003
2033	$25,000	$1,279,003	$115,110	**$1,394,113**

$30,000 Per Year

Year	Amount Invested	Plus Prev. Year's Total	Plus 9% Return	Grand Total
2014	$30,000	$0	$2,700	$32,700
2015	$30,000	$62,700	$5,643	$68,343
2016	$30,000	$98,343	$8,851	$107,194
2017	$30,000	$137,194	$12,347	$149,541
2018	$30,000	$179,541	$16,159	$195,700
2019	$30,000	$225,700	$20,313	$246,013
2020	$30,000	$276,013	$24,841	$300,854
2021	$30,000	$330,854	$29,777	$360,631
2022	$30,000	$390,631	$35,157	$425,788
2023	$30,000	$455,788	$41,021	$496,809
2024	$30,000	$526,809	$47,413	$574,222
2025	$30,000	$604,222	$54,380	$658,602
2026	$30,000	$688,602	$61,974	$750,576
2027	$30,000	$780,576	$70,252	$850,827
2028	$30,000	$880,827	$79,274	**$960,102**
2029	$30,000	$990,102	$89,109	$1,079,211
2030	$30,000	$1,109,211	$99,829	$1,209,040
2031	$30,000	$1,239,040	$111,514	$1,350,554
2032	$30,000	$1,380,554	$124,250	$1,504,804
2033	$30,000	$1,534,804	$138,132	**$1,672,936**

Rounding off the results in the chart, 20 years' worth of investments comes to:

- $836,000 based on investing $15,000 per year
- $1.1 million based on investing $20,000 per year
- $1.4 million based on investing $25,000 per year
- $1.7 million based on investing $30,000 per year

Simply eliminate the last five years on the chart to see where your nest egg would stand after 15 years of saving. In this case the rounded-off results come to:

- $480,000 based on investing $15,000 per year
- $640,000 based on investing $20,000 per year
- $800,000 based on investing $25,000 per year
- $960,000 based on investing $30,000 per year

Keep in mind these results are irrespective of the equity building in your home, a sizable portion of which can be added to the totals shown above, assuming you are willing to downsize after retiring.

This should begin to give you a rough idea of the average amount you'll need to save each year in order to reach your goal. Of course this is simply a hypothetical example. It's highly unlikely you'll be able to save exactly the same dollar amount per year from the beginning to the end of your working career, and it's pretty much a guarantee the stock market won't consistently return the same percentage year in and year out.

Far more likely, you'll begin by investing small amounts early on, then watch those amounts grow – hopefully dramatically – as your salary grows. This was the case for us. Meanwhile, the stock market will have good years and bad, but hopefully it will balance out in the end to something close to long-term historical averages.

Exercise #2: Investing Different Amounts Each Year

Now let's engage in another hypothetical exercise, this one mixing in a certain amount of real-world data based on our own experience. In this exercise we'll use *actual* dollar amounts we invested each year for 15 years, but we'll plug them into a spreadsheet that assumes a consistent annual return of 9% per year. The "Grand Total" column in the following chart shows the results based on this hypothetical 9% return, while the "Actual Results" column next to it compares real-world returns received during this same period of time.

Actual Dollars Invested for 15 Years But With a Hypothetical 9% Consistent Annual Return

Year	Annual Amount Invested	Plus Prev. Year's Total	Plus 9% Return	Grand Total	Actual Results
1992	$415	$0	$0	$415	$415
1993	$833	$1,248	$112	$1,360	$1,848
1994	$4,106	$5,466	$492	$5,958	$6,578
1995	$8,312	$14,270	$1,284	$15,555	$23,413
1996	$11,680	$27,235	$2,451	$29,686	$45,122
1997	$14,305	$43,991	$3,959	$47,950	$57,721
1998	$15,811	$63,761	$5,738	$69,499	$72,042
1999	$16,114	$85,613	$7,705	$93,319	$112,339
2000	$30,066	$123,385	$11,105	$134,489	$128,276
2001	$43,948	$178,437	$16,059	$194,497	$168,203
2002	$40,020	$234,517	$21,106	$255,623	$184,314
2003	$37,858	$293,481	$26,413	$319,894	$296,000
2004	$33,361	$353,255	$31,793	$385,048	$396,529
2005	$44,353	$429,401	$38,646	$468,047	$480,222
2006	$41,127	$509,174	$45,826	**$555,000**	**$626,219**

As you can see from the chart, our yearly investment amounts fluctuated dramatically from the beginning of our investment plan to the end. They began at just a few hundred dollars per year, then ratcheted consistently higher before kicking into overdrive in 2000 following Robin's career retraining. Our average yearly investment over the entire 15-year period was slightly less than $23,000 per year.

We were surprised ourselves when we ran these numbers for the first time and saw that our actual results had outpaced a consistent 9% annual return. In fact they had outpaced a consistent 10% return, which would have resulted in $586,890. A consistent 11% return would have resulted in $620,868 – more or less in line with our actual results of $626,219.

How can we explain such a robust return? Was it simply the result of strong stock market performance during the years in which we happened to be investing?

The simple answer is yes. During the 15-year period from 1992 to 2006, the S&P 500 returned 12.02% based on simple averages and 10.66% based on compound annual growth rates (more on that in a moment). Thus our annualized return of 11% was more or less in line with the stock market as a whole.

This chart should lend some confidence that, despite fluctuating investment amounts and wildly varying rates of return through the years, real-world results really can match or even outperform hypothetical results based on a consistent 9% return.

Your investment amounts, like ours, may start out small but build over time as your salary grows. We suggest you incorporate this likely dollar progression into your financial plans. If you take our advice to heart, however, and invest in yourself first, then your investments should start out higher than ours did and remain more consistent through time than ours were. This more consistent approach has its benefits, chief among them the fact that more dollars are being invested early on, translating into more time for those dollars to compound. A more consistent approach also makes planning for the future that much easier.

Which leads us to our next topic of discussion. What annual rates of return should *you* assume when putting together your financial plan for the future?

Estimating Future Stock Market Returns

When we began investing in the mid-1990s, people were almost manically upbeat about the stock market. The idea that we were in a new era of investing was very much in the air. We were in the midst of multiple back-to-back years of 20%+ returns and there seemed to be no end in sight as to how high the S&P 500 could go, let alone the NASDAQ. Just take a look at these annualized returns from 1995 to 1999 to get an idea:

Year	S&P 500	NASDAQ
1995	38.0%	39.9%
1996	23.1%	22.7%
1997	33.7%	21.6%
1998	28.7%	39.6%
1999	21.1%	85.6%

Don't we all wish we could have *those* five years of returns back again! In 1999 the NASDAQ returned an astonishing 85% – and that was after four years of 20% to 40% gains. No wonder people thought we were in a new era of investing – or else in the midst of one of the biggest investment bubbles of all times.

I remember reading articles in financial magazines about "Dow 30,000" and "Dow 40,000," and the articles were not written tongue in cheek. To this day a book is available on Amazon.com called *Dow 30,000 by 2008!: Why It's Different This Time*. First published in 2003 by a chartered financial analyst after the dot-com boom had already gone bust, it claimed a return to good times was just around the corner. We all know how that prediction turned out.

I still have an article from *Kiplinger's* dated January 1995 that claims an average annual return of 15% over the long run is a reasonable expectation for individuals who invest regularly in a diversified portfolio of small-cap growth stocks. Back then, talk of 15% average annual returns didn't seem so far-fetched, and when you look at the returns shown above you can begin to understand why. I went on to write in my journal, "If this is so, my calculations may be overly conservative. I've based my expectations on an average annual return of 9%."

Because of articles like this one, I bumped my estimates up to 10% and still felt like I was being hopelessly pessimistic. Nowadays if I were to suggest annualized returns of 10%, many would say I was being hopelessly optimistic.

What the Historical Record Shows

You have to make assumptions when planning for the future, there's simply no way around it. As long as your assumptions have a basis in fact – and not just over the short term but over the long term – you're on relatively solid ground. But it would be a mistake to assume 20% annualized stock market returns just because you're lucky enough to experience a 20% return in any given year, or even in a string of years. Why? Because the historical record simply doesn't support it.

What the historical record does support is the probability of stock market returns in the 8% to 10% range over the long term. Does that mean you're definitely going to get those returns during the years in which you are actively investing? No, of course not. But you've got to start somewhere, and as good a place to start as any is with the historical returns of the stock market over a very long period of time – say, from before the Great Depression in 1929 to the present day.

Getting an accurate read on historical stock market performance is a surprisingly tricky thing in its own right. You'd think everyone would agree in hindsight, for example, on what the annualized returns have been for the S&P 500. After all, the S&P 500 is an index of the 500 biggest and best-capitalized companies in the U.S. Nevertheless, different websites post slightly different annualized returns for the same year, although most are in rough agreement.

We rely on data posted by moneychimp.com under their helpful feature called "CAGR of the Stock Market: Annualized Returns of the S&P 500." CAGR stands for "compound annual growth rate" and their "CAGR-lator" makes it possible to enter any range of years during the entire history of the S&P 500 and instantly see the annualized growth rate for that period.

According to their website, from 1871 to 2012, the longest possible range to date, the S&P 500's annualized return (dividends included) has been 10.60% based on taking the simple average – that is, adding up each year's annual return percentage then dividing it by the total number of years.

The Problem With Using Simple Averages

Using the simple average seems straightforward enough, doesn't it? However, it isn't always the best approach. Let's look at an extreme example to illustrate. Let's say you have $10,000 invested in a particular stock and you make 100% on your investment in the first year. That means you made $10,000 on your investment, leaving you with a new total of $20,000.

Now let's say you lose 50% of that investment the next year. That's a loss of $10,000, putting you right back where you started at $10,000. Your real annualized gain is zero since you started and ended at the same dollar amount. However, the simple average would suggest your annual return was 25%. Why? Because (100% gain - 50% loss) ÷ 2 = 25%. We intuitively see this doesn't make practical sense – and that's where compound annual growth rates (CAGR) come in handy.

Why Compound Annual Growth Rates Are More Reliable

A compound annual growth rate essentially shows the rate at which an investment would have grown *if* it grew at a steady rate. By using the geometric mean rather than the arithmetic mean it provides a truer picture of actual returns. Unfortunately, calculating the CAGR is no easy matter unless you're a math whiz or happen to have a financial calculator on hand. If you want to know the equation, here it is:

$$CAGR = (\text{Ending Value} / \text{Beginning Value})^{((1 / n) - 1)}$$
where n is the length of time of the investment in years

Calculating a fractional exponent is not something you can easily do on an ordinary calculator. However, websites like moneychimp.com and investopedia.com now offer CAGR calculators you can use. For our purposes, the important thing to understand is that calculations based on CAGR provide a more accurate assessment of long-term annualized returns, and that's what our focus is on here.

According to moneychimp.com, the annualized return of the S&P 500 from 1871 to 2012 based on compound annual growth rates is **8.92%**. The CAGR is usually a percent or two less than the simple average (which you may recall was 10.60%). Inflation-adjusted annualized returns over this same period were 6.71% based on the CAGR.

What Annual Rate of Return Should You Use?

The S&P 500 is a reasonable proxy for the entire U.S. stock market, so it would be fair to say that, over the long run, the stock market has had an annualized return of approximately 9% and an inflation-adjusted return of approximately 7%. If you want to plan for the future, you could do worse than basing your assumptions on these percentages.

Now if you're optimistic by nature, you can assume stock market returns of 10% or possibly even 11% per year and still be more or less in range of what the historical record supports. But going much higher than that might start to look more like wishful thinking than conscientious planning.

When putting together your own financial plan for the future, we suggest you use a percentage rate of between 8% and 10% per year if you are investing primarily in the stock market, with **9%** being the obvious middle ground assumption. Some will say this is too high, others too low, but at least it is in the ball park. Keep in mind a 9% return is based on investing the bulk of your money in stocks during your primary investing years. If you wish to invest more conservatively, with bonds making up 25% or more of your portfolio, you may want to assume a slightly lower annual rate of return.

You may be wondering whether you should use inflation-adjusted returns when making assumptions about future investment growth. (Inflation-adjusted returns are usually about two percentage points lower than unadjusted returns.) With regard to your personal investment plan we would say no, and here's why: you already factored in inflation (i.e., by adding 2% per year) when calculating your future retirement income needs. That means your nest egg has already been adjusted *upwards* to account for inflation. Adjusting annual returns *downwards* as well would be to account for inflation twice.

Even if the assumptions you make about future stock market returns aren't totally correct (and there's a good chance they won't be), the mere fact that you have made a plan and adhered to it means you're ahead of the game and almost assuredly better off than you would have been otherwise.

Market Resilience

It's a comfort to remember that the stock market has survived and thrived despite such catastrophic events as the Stock Market Crash of 1929, the ensuing Great Depression, and two World Wars. It puts into perspective the concerns of our own time and makes us realize the markets are surprisingly resilient over the long term. Returns may be flatter than we would like, or even negative for a period of time, but over the very long term the markets have always bounced back and proven themselves quite robust.

For anyone just beginning to invest today, it's also something of a comfort to realize that the Great Recession has wrung some risk out of the markets. During the five-year period from 2008 to 2012, the S&P 500 returned just 1.63% based on the compound annual growth rate (or -0.17% when adjusted for inflation). This suggests stocks may offer a better value than they did before the recession, which could bode well for the future. Markets may (and we emphasize may) outperform in the years to come, bringing annual returns more in line with long-term historical averages.

Preparing Your Investment Spreadsheet

Now that you've had a chance to examine some hypothetical spreadsheet examples and consider the probable rates of return you should use, it's time to prepare your own investment spreadsheet. This spreadsheet will serve as your master plan going forward. It will track your taxable, 401(k), and Roth IRA investments and will include a Grand Total column so you can quickly see where you stand at the end of each year.

Once your spreadsheet is set up, all you have to do is revisit it once a year to assess how you're doing against plan. You'll update it at that point to include actual results instead of estimates for the year just past. That will increase the accuracy and relevancy of your plan going forward.

We urge you not to skip this step even if the word spreadsheet gives you chills. We promise to keep it simple. More importantly, we offer a spreadsheet template online if you'd prefer not build the template from scratch. (And why would you?)

To avail yourself of this shortcut, simply visit our website at **wherewebe.com** and download the Excel spreadsheet template under the "Early Retirement" tab. It's the same template we present here, and it already has all of the columns and formulas set up for you. There's even a helpful instruction sheet on a separate tab within the document.

You'll still need to go into the spreadsheet itself, of course, and manually enter the dollar amounts you expect to invest each year, but this is a simple matter of data entry. Once this is done, the spreadsheet is tailored to your situation and you can begin tweaking it to play with different investment scenarios.

A First Look at the Sample Spreadsheet

We created the following investment spreadsheet to guide us on our own journey to early retirement. Because we found it genuinely useful, we wanted to share it with you too.

Sample Investment Spreadsheet
(9% Annual Return)

	TAXABLE					401(k)	
Year	Amount Invested	+ Prev. Year Total	Annual % Return	Total Taxable	Amount Invested	401(k) Match	+ Prev. Year Total
2013				$0			
2014	$2,000	$2,000	$180	$2,180	$4,000	$2,000	$6,000
2015	$3,000	$5,180	$466	$5,646	$4,000	$2,000	$12,540
2016	$4,000	$9,646	$868	$10,514	$4,000	$2,000	$19,669
2017	$5,000	$15,514	$1,396	$16,911	$4,000	$2,000	$27,439
2018	$6,000	$22,911	$2,062	$24,973	$4,000	$2,000	$35,908
2019	$7,000	$31,973	$2,878	$34,850	$5,000	$2,500	$46,640
2020	$8,000	$42,850	$3,857	$46,707	$5,000	$2,500	$58,338
2021	$9,000	$55,707	$5,014	$60,720	$5,000	$2,500	$71,088
2022	$10,000	$70,720	$6,365	$77,085	$5,000	$2,500	$84,986
2023	$11,000	$88,085	$7,928	$96,013	$5,000	$2,500	$100,135
2024	$12,000	$108,013	$9,721	$117,734	$6,000	$3,000	$118,147
2025	$13,000	$130,734	$11,766	$142,500	$6,000	$3,000	$137,780
2026	$14,000	$156,500	$14,085	$170,585	$6,000	$3,000	$159,180
2027	$15,000	$185,585	$16,703	$202,288	$6,000	$3,000	$182,506
2028	$16,000	$218,288	$19,646	$237,933	$6,000	$3,000	$207,932
2029	$17,000	$254,933	$22,944	$277,877	$7,000	$3,500	$237,146
2030	$18,000	$295,877	$26,629	$322,506	$7,000	$3,500	$268,989
2031	$19,000	$341,506	$30,736	$372,242	$7,000	$3,500	$303,698
2032	$20,000	$392,242	$35,302	$427,544	$7,000	$3,500	$341,531
2033	$21,000	$448,544	$40,369	$488,913	$7,000	$3,500	$382,769

		ROTH IRA				
Annual % Return	Total 401(k)	Amount Invested	+ Prev. Year Total	Annual % Return	Total Roth IRA	GRAND TOTAL
	$0				$0	$0
$540	$6,540	$4,000	$4,000	$360	$4,360	$13,080
$1,129	$13,669	$4,000	$8,360	$752	$9,112	$28,427
$1,770	$21,439	$4,000	$13,112	$1,180	$14,293	$46,246
$2,469	$29,908	$4,000	$18,293	$1,646	$19,939	$66,758
$3,232	$39,140	$4,000	$23,939	$2,154	$26,093	$90,206
$4,198	$50,838	$5,000	$31,093	$2,798	$33,892	$119,579
$5,250	$63,588	$5,000	$38,892	$3,500	$42,392	$152,687
$6,398	$77,486	$5,000	$47,392	$4,265	$51,657	$189,863
$7,649	$92,635	$5,000	$56,657	$5,099	$61,756	$231,476
$9,012	$109,147	$5,000	$66,756	$6,008	$72,765	$277,924
$10,633	$128,780	$6,000	$78,765	$7,089	$85,853	$332,367
$12,400	$150,180	$6,000	$91,853	$8,267	$100,120	$392,800
$14,326	$173,506	$6,000	$106,120	$9,551	$115,671	$459,762
$16,426	$198,932	$6,000	$121,671	$10,950	$132,621	$533,841
$18,714	$226,646	$6,000	$138,621	$12,476	$151,097	$615,677
$21,343	$258,489	$7,000	$158,097	$14,229	$172,326	$708,692
$24,209	$293,198	$7,000	$179,326	$16,139	$195,465	$811,170
$27,333	$331,031	$7,000	$202,465	$18,222	$220,687	$923,960
$30,738	$372,269	$7,000	$227,687	$20,492	$248,179	$1,047,991
$34,449	$417,218	$7,000	$255,179	$22,966	$278,145	$1,184,276

As you can see, there are separate categories for taxable, 401(k), and Roth IRA accounts. We'll talk more about each type of account in Chapter 12, but for now suffice it to say that there are significant tax advantages to 401(k) and Roth IRA accounts that make them valuable to virtually every person planning for retirement.

Any changes you make to the spreadsheet are instantly reflected in the bottom line. For instance, if you change the annual rate of return from 9% to 10%, you can instantly watch your totals increase. If you adjust your taxable investment amounts from $5,000 to $10,000 per year, you can see how your nest egg at the bottom of the spreadsheet immediately grows bigger.

Don't feel limited by the sample numbers included in the spreadsheet; they are simply illustrative and have no more bearing on our own reality than they do on yours. As you may recall from our earlier hypothetical example, our actual investments were much more erratic (to put it mildly) than the careful progression of numbers shown here. Our annual investment amounts ranged from negligible at the beginning of our plan to substantial at the end, so don't artificially limit what your own investment picture has to look like.

Make Your Spreadsheet a Living Document

We encourage you to think of your master plan not as a single document set in stone but as a flexible document that can be altered and fine-tuned at will. The idea is to play with different scenarios until you arrive at one that feels right to you. If your material situation changes, you can alter the spreadsheet to reflect your new reality, thus keeping it current and relevant to your life. Earlier iterations of your plan can always be saved for the record, but make sure this year's plan is as accurate to your real-world situation as possible.

A spreadsheet with no applicability to your real life frankly misses the whole point. If you thought you could save $10,000 per year but it quickly becomes apparent you cannot, don't abandon your plan altogether. Instead, simply alter it to make it fit what you *can* do. Try halving your goal to $5,000 per year. See if that works better for your current situation. You can always raise your investment goals later on. It's better to aim a little lower – especially early on when you're trying to create good investing habits – than to get discouraged altogether and give up.

Modifying Your Spreadsheet

If you already have a rudimentary understanding of Excel, then the practical tips that follow should be enough to guide you through how to modify and update the spreadsheet. Otherwise, detailed instructions are provided in Appendix B. That appendix also provides information on how to create your own spreadsheet from scratch should you prefer to do so.

The default spreadsheet shows 20 years' worth of data (plus a top row for any beginning investment amounts). If you only want a 15-year plan, simply delete the bottom five rows that you don't need. Be sure to select the *entire* row you want to delete (e.g., by clicking on the row number at the far left then hitting delete).

To create a 25-year plan, copy the last five rows, put your cursor on the appropriate cell (e.g., A30), then paste to add five more rows to the bottom of the spreadsheet. Again, be sure to select the *entire* rows you want to copy and paste.

You can manually update the years in the "**Year**" column simply by clicking on the cells you want to change, typing in the correct information, and hitting enter.

If you have already begun saving for retirement before reading this book, then change the zeros in the top row of data to the correct amounts. The "Grand Total" number at the end of the row will automatically update.

The shaded "**Amount Invested**" columns are the primary columns you will need to update to make the spreadsheet your own. Manually enter the amounts you plan to invest each year in your taxable, 401(k), and Roth IRA accounts. These columns currently contain sample data only, but they need to reflect how much *you* actually intend to invest from one year to the next. Plug in different amounts and see how the spreadsheet automatically updates. As the numbers change, so do the totals at the bottom of the spreadsheet.

Most of the other columns in the spreadsheet update automatically and do not require inputs from you. However, you can adjust the "**Annual % Return**" columns in order to test out different return scenarios. These columns are all set to a default of 9%, but if you'd like to use a lower or higher percentage you can easily do that. Double-click on the cell you want to update and simply change the number – for example, from the default 0.09 (for 9%) to 0.08 (for 8%) or 0.1 (for 10%) or any other percent you wish to experiment with. After you've done this once, you can copy and paste this cell information to all of the other cells below it to apply the same percentage rate to those cells.

The only other column you might wish to update is the "**401(k) Match**" column. This column automatically calculates a 401(k) match for you. The default is set to 50% of the amount in the column prior to it. Many employers match their employees' 401(k) contributions at fifty cents to the dollar, although others are more generous and match dollar for dollar. The percentage can be adjusted to bring it in line with the particulars of your 401(k) plan. Double-click on the first cell you would like to update and change the percentage – for example, from "0.5" (50%) to "1.0" (100%). You can then copy and paste this cell to all other applicable cells below it.

Getting to Your Nest Egg Amount

Your ultimate goal in using the investment spreadsheet is to plug in numbers until you see the nest egg amount you arrived at in Chapter 9 ("Calculate Your Nest Egg") appear in the Grand Total column across from the year in which you ideally wish to retire. Playing with the numbers and percentages can help you figure out how best to achieve that goal.

If your earn enough to be able to invest sizable amounts of money each year, the process may be relatively straightforward and you may be done in no time. But for the rest of us, it may take a bit more time and effort.

You may realize, for instance, that you have to save a lot more than you thought you did in order to reach your goal. At that point you have some important decisions to make. You can either keep your ambitious yearly objectives in place and commit to working even harder to achieve them, or you can increase your time horizon (e.g., from 15 to 20 years) to give yourself more time to reach your goal, or you can reconsider your annual income needs in retirement and start thinking creatively about how to retire on less.

All options are on the table at this point. Don't take it all too seriously: a playful and experimental attitude will help you more than a stressed-out and frustrated one. Try on different approaches like trying on different hats and see which one fits you best. Retiring early is not a one-size-fits-all solution. Your solution needs to be tailored to fit your own circumstances and needs.

What-If Scenarios

Since none of us can read the future, it makes sense to experiment with different what-if scenarios to see how they might affect you down the road. What if your investments only return 8% instead of 9%? Can you still reach your goals? What if they return 11% or 12% instead? Why not test it out and see? What if your job prospects improve dramatically and you start investing double what you thought you could halfway through your investment years? Such was the case for us. Why not run a what-if scenario that assumes a doubling of investment amounts halfway through your plan and see how it affects your results?

After you've read Chapter 12, which discusses allocating money between taxable, 401(k), and Roth IRA accounts, you may want to revisit your spreadsheet and try experimenting with different allocations to get a better handle on how best to apportion your money and reach your goal.

Is My Goal Achievable?

Once you've plugged in numbers that let you reach your goal in the time you'd like, then you have to ask yourself the all-important question: Is this really achievable for me given my current situation? Can I *really* save $10,000 next year?

Because in the end your numbers have to be grounded in reality if this is to be more than just an exercise in number crunching. They have to jive with your real-world circumstances. So start to think about where that $10,000 is really going to come from next year.

Perhaps you have a 401(k) plan at work and you can automatically deposit 10% or more of your paycheck directly into that. And perhaps you can set up automatic payments from your checking account into a Roth IRA account each month. How much can you really spare each month without pushing things too far? Remember, this is a marathon, not a sprint, so you don't want to push so hard you make yourself or your family miserable.

If you begin to sense your preferred scenario, however delightful in its outcome, is overambitious in terms of its day-to-day demands on you or your family, try backing off a bit. Lower your investment amounts in the early years and see how that affects your overall retirement plan.

Maybe 15 years is simply too ambitious for the time being and you'll have to settle for 20 years – at least until your material circumstances change for the better. Remember, whatever plan you arrive at, it's not set in stone. You may reluctantly decide to aim for 20 years only to get an unexpected promotion at work, and suddenly 15 years is back on the table. That's the time to pull out your spreadsheet and have another look.

Let your actual life dictate the numbers you plug into your spreadsheet, especially during the early years. Tie them to reality. Try to imagine really saving the amount you see on paper in the coming year, and if you can do that and feel good about it, then that is a true number that has real value to you and your situation.

If, on the other hand, next year's number makes you cringe, then it's back to the drawing board. Try a smaller number until you can look at it without feeling panicky. In the end you want a number that doesn't make your palms sweat!

Getting Buy-In on Your Investment Plan

This is as good a time as any to mention the importance of involving your spouse or significant other in the early retirement planning process. It's awfully hard to go it alone when it comes to saving for early retirement – unless you happen to be well and truly single. If you're a couple, then the two of you should ideally be on the same page.

Teamwork and Compromise

We encourage you either to look at the spreadsheet together and try different scenarios as a team – or else share the results of two or three different scenarios with your spouse and get input and buy-in early on. See if he or she is on board with your general approach. If you get the sense your plans are too aggressive from their standpoint, see what you can do to tone them down a bit.

Hopefully your spouse will be as excited as you are about the idea of retiring early, but if not, you may have to come up with a compromise solution. Be sure to let your spouse know how important the idea of early retirement is to you, but also try to be flexible about specific retirement dates and yearly investment amounts.

If your spouse genuinely doesn't want to retire early like you do, that doesn't mean you necessarily have to abandon your plans altogether. In fact it could make planning for retirement easier instead of harder. If he or she genuinely prefers to continue working and isn't unduly put out at the thought of your retiring early, then you may need to save less than you otherwise would have. Your spouse will continue to receive a salary, so a less rigorous schedule of investing may be needed – which could be better solution for both of you.

Early Retirement as a Shared Goal

In the early days of our retirement planning, Robin thought she wanted to continue working even after I retired early. She supported my desire because she could see how important it was to me, and she was even willing to make some sacrifices so we could save more and help make that dream come true. So I plugged numbers into the first iteration of our spreadsheet and before long we were off and running. We invested small amounts at first, but at least it was a beginning.

A few years into the plan, Robin came to the realization she wanted to retire early too. At that point I pulled the spreadsheet out again and looked at it with fresh eyes. I experimented with different scenarios and rejiggered it to allow for the possibility of both of us retiring early.

At first the results weren't promising. Our salaries were so low I simply couldn't make the numbers add up. But we both kept thinking and talking about it until we arrived at a solution. Robin would need to retrain and get a job that paid more than her travel agent job currently did. Her higher salary would allow us both to retire at the same time. Meanwhile I would do what I could to improve my own prospects at work to get us to our goal faster.

From that day forward we began talking and thinking about early retirement as a shared goal, one for which we were both willing to work hard. It meant big changes in terms of our jobs and our spending habits, but it also gave us something meaningful to focus on and get excited about in the not-so-distant future. We would go on hikes on weekends and talk excitedly about the travel possibilities in our future once jobs no longer tied us to a single place.

Our investment spreadsheet became our roadmap to the future. We could look at it and see we were making real progress from one year to the next. The dollar amounts in the Grand Total column kept going up – and they were going up faster each year as our annual investment amounts increased and compounding began to make a real difference

At the end of each year I would update the spreadsheet and we would have a look at it together and see where we stood. It was an exciting time, and all the more so because it was shared.

Updating Your Spreadsheet with Actual Results

Once your spreadsheet is set up, all you have to do is revisit it once a year to assess how you're doing against plan. You'll plug in actual results at the end of each year so you can plan for future years using real numbers instead of estimates. Each year you do this, the future becomes a little less fuzzy because you have more real data to work with. Also, the window until your target retirement date continues to narrow, so there are fewer years in which you have to rely on educated guesswork to get to your goal.

Taking a Year-End Snapshot

Here is the approach we take to updating the spreadsheet at the end of each calendar year. On December 31 we take a "snapshot" of our investments at that moment in time. We add up each category of investment separately – taxable, 401(k), and Roth IRA. Then we plug those amounts into the top row of the spreadsheet, replacing the estimated subtotals with real data. We delete all the formulas and estimates in that row and replace them with a single typed-in number instead – one for taxable, one for 401(k), and one for Roth IRA. The Grand Total number updates automatically, but we usually replace it anyway with a hard number instead of a formula to give it a sense of finality.

Updating the Spreadsheet Annually: An Example

Let's say it's December 31, 2014 and the markets have posted their final numbers for the year. At that point 2014 is no longer an unknown but a known, so you can plug in actual results. On that day you take a snapshot of your portfolio, adding up the subtotals for each type of investment, plugging them into the top row of the spreadsheet, and deleting all the extraneous formulas and estimates in the process. Up until now the first five rows of your spreadsheet have looked like this (note: we have deleted the 401(k) columns for readability purposes):

		TAXABLE					ROTH IRA			GRAND
Year	Amount Invested	+ Prev. Year Total	Annual % Return	Total Taxable	Amount Invested	+ Prev. Year Total	Annual % Return	Total Roth IRA		TOTAL
2014	$2,000	$2,000	$180	$2,180	$4,000	$4,000	$360	$4,360		$13,080
2015	$3,000	$5,180	$466	$5,646	$4,000	$8,360	$752	$9,112		$28,427
2016	$4,000	$9,646	$868	$10,514	$4,000	$13,112	$1,180	$14,293		$46,246
2017	$5,000	$15,514	$1,396	$16,911	$4,000	$18,293	$1,646	$19,939		$66,758
2018	$6,000	$22,911	$2,062	$24,973	$4,000	$23,939	$2,154	$26,093		$90,206

Now they look like this:

		TAXABLE					ROTH IRA			GRAND
Year	Amount Invested	+ Prev. Year Total	Annual % Return	Total Taxable	Amount Invested	+ Prev. Year Total	Annual % Return	Total Roth IRA		TOTAL
2014				$2,664				$4,483		$14,355
2015	$3,000	$5,664	$510	$6,174	$4,000	$8,483	$763	$9,246		$29,817
2016	$4,000	$10,174	$916	$11,089	$4,000	$13,246	$1,192	$14,439		$47,760
2017	$5,000	$16,089	$1,448	$17,537	$4,000	$18,439	$1,659	$20,098		$68,409
2018	$6,000	$23,537	$2,118	$25,656	$4,000	$24,098	$2,169	$26,267		$92,006

Notice how the row for 2014 now only has a few numbers on it. All the other data has been deleted. The numbers are hard numbers that have been typed in rather than being based on formulas, and any data from previous years has been eliminated from the chart. The year 2014 is now the beginning year on this current iteration of the spreadsheet.

Notice, too, how all the subtotal dollar amounts in the years below 2014 are different from what they were before. That's because the actual 2014 data has rolled forward into the estimated data for future years.

Comparing the two spreadsheets, you can quickly tell you're ahead of plan. That's great news, of course. When you look at the bottom line of your spreadsheet, you can see the Grand Total number still meets or exceeds your desired nest egg.

Tracking Your Progress

Tracking your progress lets you fine-tune your plan along the way and monitor if you are still on course to retire by your target date. We encourage you to take a good hard look at your spreadsheet at least once a year in order to compare actual performance against plan. Give some careful attention as to how best to proceed based on the actual facts in front of you.

What If You're Ahead of Schedule?

Being ahead of schedule is a fine problem to have: enjoy your good fortune. If your material situation has changed for the better – if you've received a substantial raise at work, for example – now might be a good time to consider raising your annual investment amounts for the years to come. By doing so you might discover you can retire even sooner than expected, or else that you're going to have a larger nest egg than you thought you would. Either prospect is quite wonderful to consider.

What If You're Behind Schedule?

If you're just a little off course in any given year, there's no need to worry. That may simply be the result of poor market conditions over the short term, something over which you have virtually no control. If you're in a bear market, then it's hardly surprising you aren't reaching your expected goals for the year. But that's all right, you should tell yourself, because you're buying more shares of stock at a lower price than you could have otherwise. In the bull market years that typically follow after a bear market, your returns are likely to exceed expectations, and in those years you should be able to make up for lost ground.

Our thought process during bear markets was simply to shrug our shoulders and say, "Well, we did everything we planned to do for the year. We met our personal goals in terms of the amounts we invested. The rest is up to the markets." The key as far as we were concerned was not to get discouraged or make abrupt changes because of a panicky feeling we needed to *do* something. Instead, we needed to stay the course and continue investing according to plan. As long as we kept doing the things we knew were right to do and that were in our control to do, the rest was a matter of having faith in the long-term tendency of the markets to go up rather than down.

What If You're Way Off Track?

If you're way off track and have significantly less saved up than you thought you would by the end of a particular year or string of years, then you have some serious thinking to do.

First, try to determine why you fell short of your goals. Did you invest as much as you had hoped to? If not, perhaps your goals were simply too ambitious. You may need to bring them more into line with what you can actually accomplish and adjust your master plan accordingly.

On the other hand, perhaps the markets experienced a severe downturn and through no fault of your own you were blown off course from where you thought you would be by this point. In that case your yearly investment goals aren't the problem, but you still need to find a way to get back on track. It's no good wishing things were better: you have to make them so. So decide which of the following you want to do:

- Invest extra in the coming years in order to catch back up with your original goals.
- Increase your time horizon to give your investments more time to compound and grow.
- Plan to make do with less in retirement – which means rethinking your spending and lifestyle choices as you head into the future.

Of course you can always hope against hope the markets strongly outperform in the years to come and fix the problem for you. But since that is completely outside your control, it's risky to rely on – especially if you're significantly behind where you thought you would be. Better to take matters into your own hands and revise your master plan to realign it with your situation as it stands today. Otherwise you risk falling further and further behind on your goals and feeling more disheartened to the point where you simply decide to give up – and that would be a real shame. Raise or lower your goals to make them jibe with reality, but don't give up altogether or you'll be doing yourself a disservice in the long run.

Tracking Your Portfolio

You can track your portfolio performance directly on your investment firm's website, of course, but you may also want to create a simple portfolio tracker on Yahoo's Finance webpage. You can pull it up at a moment's notice without having to enter a user name and password each time since there is no sensitive information on the site. All it consists of is the mutual fund symbols and the number of shares you own. Thus it offers a quick way to check your totals and track your progress on a regular basis. The bottom portion of our portfolio tracker, showing our taxable investments and our grand total, looks like this:

VFIAX	Vanguard 500 Index Admiral	06:24pm EDT	144.68	720.845	$104,291.85	↑$583.88	↑0.56%
VEXAX	Vanguard Extended Market Idx Adm	06:24pm EDT	51.61	2,076.085	$107,146.75	↑$871.96	↑0.82%
VTIAX	Vanguard Total Intl Stock Index Admiral	06:24pm EDT	26.05	3,242.82	$84,475.46	↑$713.42	↑0.85%
VBTLX	Vanguard Total Bond Market Index Adm	06:24pm EDT	10.97	18,306.98	$200,827.58	$0.00	0.00%
	Company Stock	04:00pm EDT	46.02	357.670459	$16,459.99	↑$85.84	↑0.52%
Total					$851,777.22	↑$5,066.74	↑0.60%

To create your own portfolio tracker, go to Yahoo's Finance site, click on "My Portfolios," and select "Create Portfolio." Give your new portfolio a name (we call ours "Total") and begin adding mutual fund symbols to it, followed by the number of shares you own for each. Hit save and you're good to go. Just click on "Add/Edit Holdings" if you want to change or update any information.

The only downside to portfolio trackers like this is that you have to periodically update the share information if you want to keep it current. The share amounts don't automatically update as they will on your own investment firm's website.

Keeping a Record of Performance

We recommend you save a copy of your investment spreadsheet each year before making any changes to it. That way you have a backup in case something should go wrong. It also gives you a handy historical record if you should ever want to compare your current spreadsheet to ones from previous years. We keep our spreadsheets in a financial folder on our computer and label each one by year: spreadsheet_2014, spreadsheet_2015, and so on. Keeping one spreadsheet for each year gives you a solid record of where you've been and where you're going.

Tracking Cumulative Goals vs. Actuals

When you first establish your yearly goals, you may want to create a chart that lets you compare cumulative goals vs. cumulative actuals. Our original chart is shown on the next page, followed by the same chart after it had been filled in with actuals year by year until we retired in 2006. Totals include stocks, bonds, and cash but not home equity.

The goals listed in both charts are identical, although you may have noticed the original chart extends out to 2008 and the final one only to 2006. That's because we were able to retire two years earlier than originally planned due to salaries and investment amounts in the latter half of our plan that were significantly higher than anything we could have anticipated back in 1994. This just goes to show that no plan is perfect. Your initial plan represents a beginning only, so don't expect precision of it beyond a year or two into the future.

Cumulative Goals vs. Actuals

Year	Taxable		401(k) / Roth IRA		Grand Total	
	Goal	Actual	Goal	Actual	Goal	Actual
1994	$2,500		$4,000		$6,500	
1995	$5,600		$12,628		$18,228	
1996	$11,872		$21,959		$33,831	
1997	$18,897		$32,644		$51,541	
1998	$26,764		$44,853		$71,617	
1999	$35,576		$58,776		$94,352	
2000	$45,445		$74,626		$120,071	
2001	$56,498		$92,641		$149,140	
2002	$68,878		$113,090		$181,969	
2003	$82,744		$136,273		$219,017	
2004	$101,073		$162,527		$263,600	
2005	$121,602		$192,228		$313,829	
2006	$144,594		$225,798		$370,392	
2007	$170,345		$263,713		$434,058	
2008	$199,187		$306,502		$505,688	

Cumulative Goals vs. Actuals

Year	Taxable		401(k) / Roth IRA		Grand Total	
	Goal	Actual	Goal	Actual	Goal	Actual
1994	$2,500	$2,533	$4,000	$4,045	$6,500	$6,578
1995	$5,600	$10,229	$12,628	$13,184	$18,228	$23,413
1996	$11,872	$20,090	$21,959	$25,032	$33,831	$45,122
1997	$18,897	$26,193	$32,644	$31,528	$51,541	$57,721
1998	$26,764	$29,988	$44,853	$42,054	$71,617	$72,042
1999	$35,576	$41,895	$58,776	$70,444	$94,352	$112,339
2000	$45,445	$53,977	$74,626	$74,299	$120,071	$128,276
2001	$56,498	$83,609	$92,641	$84,594	$149,140	$168,203
2002	$68,878	$97,954	$113,090	$86,360	$181,969	$184,314
2003	$82,744	$159,325	$136,273	$136,675	$219,017	$296,000
2004	$101,073	$213,683	$162,527	$182,846	$263,600	$396,529
2005	$121,602	$259,412	$192,228	$220,810	$313,829	$480,222
2006	$144,594	$347,540	$225,798	$278,679	$370,392	$626,219

Note: Values do not include home equity

A chart like the one above is instructive in that it provides a series of snapshots in time, the first taken at the beginning of your plan, the rest taken at intervals one year apart. While your spreadsheet is a living document – one you should modify to keep relevant to your life – the chart above is simply a historical record of your progress.

Tracking Annual Investment Amounts

The final numbers you may want to track are your annual investment amounts (goal vs. actual). A simple chart like the one below should do the trick. These are sample numbers only, of course; you should enter your own goal numbers from the spreadsheet you create.

Annual Investment Amounts – Goal vs. Actual

Year	Taxable		401(k)		Roth IRA		Total	
	Goal	Actual	Goal	Actual	Goal	Actual	Goal	Actual
2014	$2,000		$4,000		$4,000		$10,000	
2015	$3,000		$4,000		$4,000		$11,000	
2016	$4,000		$4,000		$4,000		$12,000	
2017	$5,000		$4,000		$4,000		$13,000	
2018	$6,000		$4,000		$4,000		$14,000	
2019	$7,000		$5,000		$5,000		$17,000	
2020	$8,000		$5,000		$5,000		$18,000	
2021	$9,000		$5,000		$5,000		$19,000	
2022	$10,000		$5,000		$5,000		$20,000	
2023	$11,000		$5,000		$5,000		$21,000	
2024	$12,000		$6,000		$6,000		$24,000	
2025	$13,000		$6,000		$6,000		$25,000	
2026	$14,000		$6,000		$6,000		$26,000	
2027	$15,000		$6,000		$6,000		$27,000	
2028	$16,000		$6,000		$6,000		$28,000	

Chapter 11.
Invest Regularly in Index Funds

Once you have prepared your investment spreadsheet, you should know exactly how much you need to invest over the coming year. Now take that amount and divide by twelve to determine the exact amount you need to invest each month in order to meet your annual goal. All that remains is to make sure you actually invest that amount each month, regardless of how the market is performing.

There should be no question from one month to the next *if* you are going to invest: *of course* you are going to invest. It doesn't matter what the markets are doing – whether they are up, down, or sideways. You have no control over that so you shouldn't concern yourself with it. But you do have control over making your monthly investments as planned. Stay true to those monthly commitments and you'll have taken your biggest step towards achieving your goal of early retirement.

Put Your Investments on Auto-Pilot

The secret to investing regularly is to put your investments on auto-pilot. If you automate the savings process, it happens without your having to think about it – and that's a good thing, because you may well be your own worst enemy when it comes to investing on a regular schedule. Things get in the way, expenses add up, money's tight, the markets are down, you're feeling discouraged, you don't want to write the check, you don't want to think about it right now, you don't have the time or the energy – the excuses the human mind can come up with not to do something are nothing short of amazing. Auto-pilot gets rid of most of those excuses.

Set It and Forget It

The best place to start automating your investments is at work. If your company offers a 401(k) plan then you should sign up for automatic deductions from your paycheck. Because the money is taken directly out of your paycheck before you ever see it, it's almost as if it never existed in the first place, so you don't miss it so much. You don't have to part with it by hand – by writing a check, say, and seeing your checkbook balance get lower. By automating the process, you've eliminated the middle man – you – from the equation.

You can also set up automatic monthly transfers directly out of your checking account into your taxable and Roth IRA accounts. You decide on the amount each month and which day of the month the transfer is made. It won't be quite as invisible as the 401(k) process because you'll see the money disappear out of your checking account each month, but at least it's hands-off and you have less to think about, which is your goal. "Set it and forget it" is a good motto when it comes to investing.

Automating your investments keeps you on the straight and narrow to your annual investment goal in a way nothing else will. Your only responsibility then becomes making sure you have sufficient funds on hand to cover the automatic transfers. Think of your monthly investments as you would your monthly mortgage payment. There's no question you're going to make that payment: it's not an option, it's a necessity. That's the mindset you want to foster.

Pay Yourself First

You've probably heard the expression "pay yourself first," which means invest in your own future first before paying other bills or expenses. That may sound a little extreme, but it gives top priority to you. Automating your payments makes it far more likely you won't skip out on a payment to yourself. It forces your hand in a way, which isn't all bad when you consider how many other things in life are calling out for you to spend money on them. The siren call of spending is a little easier to resist if you tie yourself to the mast like Odysseus and give yourself no other choice but to stay the course.

That said, be sure to leave yourself a little buffer when you select your monthly investment amount so you aren't pushing right up against the limits of what you can handle financially. Better to select a smaller amount you know you can manage month in and month out than to push too hard and find yourself strapped for cash in any given month.

Consistency is your goal, not stress and financial hardship. Let your monthly contribution to your future be a positive aspect of your life, something you can feel good about, rather than a negative burden that puts a strain on your existence.

Use Dollar Cost Averaging

Putting your investments on autopilot lets you take advantage of a technique called dollar cost averaging. With dollar cost averaging you invest an equal amount of money each month in an asset regardless of the share price, which means you end up purchasing more shares when prices are low and fewer shares when prices are high.

This approach tends to reduce your average share price over time. A lump sum invested all at once could be invested at just the wrong moment when prices are especially high. Dollar cost averaging helps insulate you against market risk to some degree because you spread your purchases out evenly over a long period of time and over a range of prices.

Let's say you decide to purchase $100 per month of a particular mutual fund for three months. In the first month the fund is valued at $50, so your fixed monthly investment of $100 buys you two shares. Next month the valuation is $33 so your $100 buys you three shares. The last month it is $25 so your $100 buys you four shares. That's nine shares altogether which you've bought for an average price of about $33 each ($300 ÷ 9). If you had invested all $300 in a lump sum in the first month, you would have paid $50 per share and only received six shares. By dollar cost averaging you have reduced your average share price and lessened the market risk that can come with investing a lump sum all at once.

Dollar cost averaging also helps offset the natural human tendency to buy an asset when it is performing well and not buy it when it is performing poorly. We all like a winner, don't we? But buying an asset when it is flying high means buying it at a higher share price. Logically we should want to buy it when it is underperforming and we can get more shares for our money, but this isn't always how human nature works. Dollar cost averaging helps us do what we should do anyway, which is buy more shares of an investment when it is "on sale" and less when it is not.

Decide on an Overall Investment Mix

One of the most important decisions you can make as an investor is selecting your overall investment mix of stocks, bonds, and cash. Your individual investments within that mix are of secondary importance to the portfolio allocation itself. Whether you buy this particular stock or that particular stock is less important than deciding how much of your portfolio should consist of stocks in the first place.

Risk Tolerance and Time Horizon

Your investment mix should be a reflection of your own risk tolerance and time horizon. Let's say you have a long time horizon and a relatively high tolerance for risk (or at least you think you do; you'll know for certain after you've ridden out your first major recession). In that case you may want to invest heavily in stocks and have just a toehold in bonds during your primary investing years, since stocks offer the greatest potential for long-term growth.

On the other hand, if you have a relatively low tolerance for risk and suspect you won't be able to sleep at night if too much of your money is riding on stocks, then you'll want to keep a more balanced portfolio of stocks, bonds, and cash to help buffer the volatility that inevitably comes with owning just stocks.

Your time horizon to retirement is particularly important to consider when determining your investment mix. A portfolio 80% to 100% invested in the stock market might make sense in your beginning and middle investing years, but as you near retirement you have less time to recover from serious downturns in the market. Certainly once you retire you need a reliable source from which to withdraw money if the stock market should nosedive, so having a solid position in bonds becomes crucial. Capital preservation and income generation become at least as important as the need for additional capital appreciation once you retire.

During our primary investing years we invested 100% (or very close to it) in stocks and stock mutual funds. Our overriding goal during those years was capital appreciation. We weren't concerned about market volatility because our time horizon was long enough at that point that we knew we could ride out whatever storms might come. In fact we viewed downturns in the market as buying opportunities, and we benefited from them once the markets bounced back and stock prices rose again.

We waited longer than was prudent, however, to carve out a significant position in bonds as we approached retirement. In fact it wasn't until we sold our home in the first year of retirement and put the money into a bond fund that we established our first meaningful position in bonds. (Although we did have $30,000 saved up in a bond fund for use over the first year of our retirement as a partial hedge against risk.)

Luckily for us things worked out, but in hindsight it would have been wiser to incrementally increase our bond holdings over the last five years leading up to retirement. Then we could have apportioned some of the money from the sale of our home to stocks and the rest to bonds based on our preferred investment mix as we entered retirement.

The Case for a More Aggressive Approach

The following table makes it clear why you should invest primarily in stocks during your early years when you still have a long time horizon until retirement. During this period you want to do everything in your power to maximize growth.

Primary Focus	Investment Mix	Average Annual Return	Years With a Loss (86 Years Total)
Growth	100% stocks	9.9%	25
Growth	80% stocks / 20% bonds	9.4%	23
Growth	70% stocks / 30% bonds	9.0%	22
Balanced	60% stocks / 40% bonds	8.6%	21
Balanced	50% stocks / 50% bonds	8.2%	17
Balanced	40% stocks / 60% bonds	7.8%	16
Income	30% stocks / 70% bonds	7.3%	14
Income	20% stocks / 80% bonds	6.7%	12
Income	100% bonds	5.6%	13

Based on historical data provided in Vanguard portfolio allocation models

The table is based on historical data from 1926 to 2011. That's 86 years' worth of data. It illustrates how your average annual return goes up as your allocation to stocks goes up – from 5.6% with an all-bonds portfolio to 9.9% with an all-stocks portfolio. It also illustrates how your *risk* goes up as your allocation to stocks goes up. Out of 86 years, you would have had to stomach 25 years with a loss if you had an all-stocks portfolio, as compared to 13 years with an all-bonds portfolio.

The table makes it clear *risk* and *reward* go hand in hand. The more risk you are willing to take on, the more reward you are likely to get. After all, if it weren't for the potentially higher returns offered by stocks over the long run, then everyone would invest in bonds or cash because those tend to be the safer investments.

Now ask yourself, When is the best time in my life to take on the most risk? The answer for most of us is, When I am young, healthy, and working full time. When better to skew your investments towards higher-risk stocks than when you are in the prime of life and fully capable of taking on such risks? You should have years and years ahead of you before you need to touch the money you're investing, so you can afford to leave it in place even if it goes down in value for a period of time as the result of a bear market.

In all likelihood you will never be better suited to taking on more risk than you are right now.

The Case for a More Conservative Approach

You might have noticed from the table that you only have to sacrifice a small amount of growth if you have a portfolio consisting of 80% stocks and 20% bonds as compared to 100% stocks. The difference in the average annual return is only 0.5% (9.9% vs. 9.4%), which isn't much, especially when you factor in the extra peace of mind those bonds may give you. Even a 70/30 stock/bond portfolio offers a very respectable average annual return of 9.0% based on historical averages.

If you are a conservative, risk-averse investor, you can take great comfort in this. It is still possible for you to take a growth-oriented stance while mitigating your risk to some degree by investing 70% in stocks and 30% in bonds. That would satisfy the need for capital appreciation during your primary investing years while still reducing some of the volatility along the way.

One could arguably do worse than setting a 70/30 portfolio mix from the very beginning and maintaining that mix through life.

If you are invested 70% or more in stocks, then you stand a good chance of reaching your early retirement goals. Much less than that, however, and you begin to get into a gray area where you can still expect to reach your goal eventually, but perhaps not as quickly as you might have otherwise.

The Risk of Being Overly Conservative

Anything less than 50% stocks and 50% bonds/cash during your primary investing years and you begin to enter what we would think of as an overly conservative space where capital appreciation takes a back seat to the perception of safety. We say perception of safety because it's a fair question whether you really are safer with an overly conservative portfolio mix. Why? Because there is more than one kind of risk when it comes to investing.

Extremely conservative investors tend to focus solely on market risk, which is the risk of losing money from fluctuations in stock market prices (i.e., if stocks go down, you lose money). A lot of people are so afraid of market risk they won't even consider investing in stocks. They would rather put all their money in a bank account earning 1% interest. They believe they're playing it safe that way.

But they're probably not adequately aware of *inflation risk*, which is the risk inflation will eat away at their investments faster than they can grow, making their money worth less and less over time. If inflation grows at 3% per year and their investments only earn 1%, then in essence they are losing 2% each and every year. Suddenly that safe bank account doesn't seem so safe any more, at least when it comes to their long-term buying power.

Once people have an understanding of inflation risk, they're generally more willing to take a second look at a balanced stock and bond portfolio. Despite the realities of market risk, the stock market on average returns about 9% per year over the long term and bonds return on average about 5% to 6% per year. Thus a well-balanced stock and bond portfolio should keep you ahead of inflation. You'll get a better real return on your investment than you would with a "safe" bank account.

Choose an Investment Firm

When we first started investing, we had investments scattered all over the map, with paperwork and electronic communications streaming in from many different directions. It was something of a relief, therefore, to switch to a simpler approach and hold just a few index funds with a single investment firm. Suddenly we could see all of our investments in a single statement and manage them with much more ease.

The Investment Firm We Chose

All of our mutual fund investments are currently with The Vanguard Group and have been since well before we retired. Vanguard is generally known for having the lowest expenses in the industry. Their average expense ratio is an extremely low 0.20% (that's one-fifth of one percent), which is 82% less than the industry average of 1.12%. That means very little is going out of your pocket into the behind-the-scenes management and operation of the funds.

We particularly like the fact Vanguard fund shareholders *own* the company. As a not-for-profit corporation, the fund's interests align naturally with those of its shareholders, who pay only what it costs Vanguard to operate the funds. There are no other parties to answer to and thus no conflicting loyalties. We think this is something special in the mutual fund industry.

Vanguard's enormous asset base – consisting of 20 million shareholder accounts with more than $1.7 trillion in U.S. mutual fund assets as of the end of 2011 – lets it take advantage of huge economies of scale. They are a big player in the financial investment world in the best sense of the word.

We receive Vanguard's email newsletters and always find their advice refreshingly straightforward. The whole world might be turning upside down as far as the TV financial news channels are concerned, but you can always count on Vanguard to counsel you to stay the course, keep a balanced portfolio, and trust in the long-term performance of the markets. Their prudent advice often runs counter to the panicky tone of the media, and that can be a comfort during difficult financial times.

Just to be clear, we have nothing to gain financially or otherwise by recommending Vanguard to you. It's simply the firm we have chosen to do our business with. There are other great firms out there – Fidelity, Charles Schwab, and T. Rowe Price among them, to name just a few. If you are already doing business with one of these firms, or with another of the many reputable investment firms out there, we aren't suggesting you go through the hassle of switching firms unless you are unhappy in some respect with the service you are receiving or the fees you are paying. But if you are just starting out and are looking for a good investment firm, we would certainly recommend Vanguard based on our own experience.

Keeping Fund Expenses Low

The average mutual fund company charges fees six times higher than Vanguard's. These fees add up over time and make a significant difference to long-term performance.

Consider this: with no fees at all, a $100,000 portfolio earning 9% per year would grow to $560,000 in 20 years. With a 1% annual fee the final value would be $458,000 – more than $100,000 less. If the annual fee were 3%, which is not out of the question with some mutual funds, the final value would only reach $305,000 – more than $250,000 less. You can see why fees matter and why we might decide to go with an investment firm like Vanguard for this reason alone.

The question of fees is even more important when it comes to bond funds. A high fee can quickly overwhelm a bond fund's performance. For example, if a bond fund returns 4% in a given year, then a 1% fee is equal to 25% of that return. If the same fund returns 1% in a given year, then a 1% fee effectively translates into a 0% return. Thus a low-return environment, whether for stocks or bonds, only increases the importance of keeping fees low.

Vanguard's ultra-low expenses apply to both stock and bond funds. To highlight just two examples, the expense ratios for its flagship Index 500 Fund and its Total Bond Market Index Fund are an astonishingly low 0.05% and 0.10% respectively. (These are the expense ratios for the preferred Admiral Shares, which require a minimum fund balance of $10,000.) It's hard to expect much better than that.

Whichever investment firm you end up choosing, we recommend you make sure their expenses are lower than the norm and that you keep your investments within that single firm as much as possible for simplicity's sake. We also recommend you compare not just the fees charged but the range of services offered by different investment firms before making a final decision as to which one is right for you. For instance, if you prefer to do most of your investing in individual stocks rather than mutual funds, you might find an online investment firm specializing in low-cost stock trades that suits your needs better than Vanguard.

Why Index Funds Make Sense

If you think of investing as primarily a means to an end and not a passion in and of itself, then index fund investing might be the right answer for you. It's a great solution if you want to keep your financial life as simple and low-maintenance as possible.

With index funds you stop trying to beat the markets and instead simply keep up with them. Index funds *mirror* the markets they track instead of trying to beat them. They replicate as closely as possible the investment weighting and returns of the benchmark index they are designed to track.

Perhaps the most famous index fund of all is also the first ever created: the Vanguard 500 Index Fund, which tracks the S&P 500 Index. It was created by John Bogle of The Vanguard Group in 1975. Vanguard is now the largest mutual fund company in the U.S., and the fund has become a mainstay of many an investment portfolio.

Built-In Diversification

When you buy an index fund, you are buying a whole portfolio of stocks in a single fund, so your risk is lower if any one of the companies in that fund should plummet in value or go out of business. The diversification provided by an index fund means your investments are spread out over many companies and usually over many asset classes. This can be a comfort to those who feel they are not quite up to the task of accurately evaluating a single company's health and financial prospects based on a balance sheet alone. Rather then betting your future on one stock or a handful of stocks, you can spread your risk over hundreds or even thousands of stocks and sleep better at night because of it.

Better Performance

Because index funds are passively managed, their fees tend to be very low, and because of that they actually tend to perform *better* over the long run than most actively managed mutual funds. This comes as something of a surprise to most people when they hear it for the first time. After all, you'd think an investment manager with all his accumulated knowledge and experience would consistently be able to beat a passively managed index fund, and yet except in rare instances this is not the case.

Why? Because the active fund manager has to charge higher fees than a passively managed index fund does. Of course the active manager expects to be paid for his services, and he also tends to trade more frequently than a passively managed fund does and thus has to cover those higher trading expenses. Over time those higher fees serve as a drag on performance — a drag the vast majority of active fund managers can't overcome over the long term. By comparison, index funds charge very low fees for the services they provide and as a result offer hard-to-beat value to the individual investor.

We like the fact index funds aren't at the mercy of any one person, no matter how well intentioned. Even a good fund manager sometimes makes bad investment choices. Then, too, active fund managers sometimes retire or change investment firms or are replaced, and the next manager may follow a considerably different and riskier investment strategy. You don't have to worry about this with a passively managed index fund. We think this makes index funds a more reliable investment over the long term.

Tax Efficiency

Index funds tend to be quite tax-efficient because share turnover is minimal. Companies are rarely added to or removed from the S&P 500, for example, so funds tracking it rarely need to buy or sell shares. That means there are fewer capital gains distributions to worry about at tax time.

Index funds are also simple to own at tax season because the mutual fund company provides you with all the information you need to report on your tax forms. Compare this to an individual stock where you are responsible for calculating and reporting the cost basis of the shares you have purchased, sometimes over a period of many years, once the shares are sold. Speaking from personal experience, we can tell you this adds unwelcome complications at tax time.

A Simpler Approach

With individual stocks it helps to be able to read and understand a balance sheet and a profit and loss statement in order to correctly assess a company's fundamental health. It takes time, effort, and skill to accurately assess a single company and its stock, decide if the stock price represents a good value, and determine not only when to buy the stock but also when to sell it. Stock index funds by comparison require fewer decisions and less analysis.

Because they are made up of hundreds (or sometimes thousands) of individual stocks, stock index funds are buy-and-hold investments that by their very nature require little in the way of personalized attention. They can only be assessed in the aggregate. You might evaluate the expense ratio of an Index 500 fund, for example, and decide whether or not the fund is a good fit for your portfolio, but it would make little sense to analyze all 500 individual companies making up the index since they are being sold as a package anyway. You couldn't take them apart even if you wanted to.

By the same token, bond index funds offer a much easier approach to investing in bonds than going through the headaches of laddering individual bonds. With a bond fund you get professional management, broad diversification, and high liquidity at very low cost. There are no fees for buying or selling shares of a no-load bond index fund, whereas the bid-ask spread to buy and sell individual bonds can be quite high. For ease of use and low cost, it's hard to beat a good bond index fund.

With index funds in general, your life doesn't have to revolve around your investments. You live your life as normal and do the things you love to do. Meanwhile your investments are working for you in the background without your having to pay much attention to them.

No more trying to beat the markets. No more spending hours reading financial magazines and trying to figure out the next hot stock or the next hot mutual fund. Simply invest it, forget it, and be done. This buy-and-hold strategy makes your life (and your taxes) much simpler. Instead of reacting to the latest market news, you insulate yourself from those concerns and focus on what you *can* control, which is your monthly contributions to the index funds you have chosen.

Ease of Access and Usability

A final benefit of mutual funds in general is that they offer wonderfully easy access when it comes to buying and selling shares, transferring shares between funds, and withdrawing money. This can be an important factor when deciding where to invest your money.

We continue to own a little stock in the company for which I worked, and each time we withdraw shares we need to pay a transaction fee to the broker and another fee to have the money wired electronically to our checking account. These fees apply each and every time we withdraw money, no matter how big or small the transaction. By comparison we can withdraw funds free of charge from Vanguard with no broker involved, and the money automatically appears in our checking account in a matter of two or three business days. Their website is easy to use and lets us complete a transaction in less than a minute or two, and we can quickly get an overview of our total portfolio holdings.

Invest in Your Core Holdings

Your core holdings are the handful of investments that form the foundation of your portfolio. They are the investments you hold onto for a lifetime. For that reason you want to make sure they are high-quality investments with a history of steady performance.

We recommend you use broadly diversified index funds as your core holdings. Just three stock index funds are enough to give you worldwide coverage for equities. You really don't need more than that! To those you should add one more fund for U.S. bonds. Here are the four fund types we recommend for your core holdings:

1. **S&P 500 Index Fund.** An index fund that mirrors the S&P 500 will give you broad exposure to the top 500 large-cap companies in the U.S. Large-cap stands for large capitalization, and these are the largest, most powerful, and most well-capitalized companies in the U.S. Together they account for about *three-fourths* of the U.S. stock market's value. It's fair to say no U.S.-based portfolio is complete without an S&P 500 index fund.

2. **Extended Market Index Fund.** An index fund that mirrors the rest of the U.S. stock market gives you broad exposure to U.S. mid-cap and small-cap stocks. Such funds typically invest in about 3,000 stocks accounting for about *one-fourth* of the market cap of the U.S. stock market. An extended market fund (or S&P completion index) is considered a complement to an S&P 500 index fund, and together the two provide exposure to the entire U.S. equity market. Mid- and small-cap markets tend to be more volatile than the large-cap market but also offer the potential for higher returns over the long run.

3. **Total International Stock Index Fund.** The world is bigger than just the U.S., so it makes sense to have exposure to the biggest, best, and fastest growing equities from other countries around the globe. Look for an index fund that gives you broad exposure to the total international stock market, including both developed and emerging economies. Emerging market stocks can be more volatile than domestic stocks, and currency risk can add even more volatility. If this is a concern for you, consider investing less in this fund than the other two equity funds.

4. **Total Bond Market Index Fund.** A balanced portfolio should include a core fund that mirrors the overall U.S. investment-grade bond market. A total bond market fund will typically invest about one-third of its assets in corporate bonds and two-thirds in U.S. government bonds of varying maturities (short-, intermediate-, and long-term). While bond funds tend to be sensitive to increases in interest rates, their overall risks are lower than stock funds.

Any major investment firm will offer index funds of these four types, so whichever firm you choose, you should be able to find good matches.

Core Vanguard Funds We Recommend

Since our own investments are with Vanguard, we provide additional details about the core Vanguard funds we own and recommend in the following table. For each fund listed there are two versions based on the amount you have to invest. The Investor Shares version requires a minimum initial investment of $3,000, while the Admiral Shares version requires $10,000 and offers a lower expense ratio. The typical investor starts in Investor Shares then transfers to Admiral Shares with a few clicks of the mouse once his or her investment crosses the $10,000 threshold.

Vanguard Fund Name	Fund Symbol and Type	Expense Ratio	Performance (10 yr)
Index 500 Fund	VFINX (Investor Shares)	0.17%	6.99%
	VFIAX (Admiral Shares)	0.05%	7.09%
Extended Market Index Fund	VEXMX (Investor Shares)	0.28%	10.58%
	VEXAX (Admiral Shares)	0.14%	10.73%
Total International Stock Index Fund	VGTSX (Investor Shares)	0.22%	9.41%
	VTIAX (Admiral Shares)	0.18%	NA
Total Bond Market Index Fund	VBMFX (Investor Shares)	0.22%	5.07%
	VBTLX (Admiral Shares)	0.10%	5.17%

If you want to own even fewer core funds, there is an easy way to do it. Instead of owning an Index 500 Fund *and* an Extended Market Fund, you can invest instead in a Total Stock Market Index Fund, which essentially combines the two into one. With one fund you gain exposure to the entire U.S. equity market, including small-, mid-, and large-cap growth and value stocks.

Percentage to Invest in Each Fund

The approach we took was to invest one third of our monthly investment amount in each of the three core equity funds described above: one third in the Index 500 fund, one third in the Extended Market fund, and one third in the International Stock fund.

At first you may have to save up enough to meet minimum deposit requirements for each fund before moving on to the next. But once all three funds are up and running, you can invest as little as $100 per month automatically into each fund from that point forward. That makes it possible to invest on a monthly basis in equal increments.

If you prefer a more risk-averse approach, you may want to invest a higher percentage in the Index 500 fund and a lower percentage in the other two. Of the three funds, the International Stock fund is probably the highest risk because it adds both currency risk and emerging market risk into the equation. Let your personal preferences guide you in terms of the specific percentages you choose to invest in each type of fund: for example, 50% Index 500, 30% Extended Market, 20% International Stock.

When your financial situation allows for it, you should also make an initial investment in a Total Bond Market index fund. If you are allocating essentially 100% to stocks during the early and middle years of your investment program, simply keep the bond fund at the minimum level for the time being. Then, about five years prior to your target retirement date, begin adding more to it.

If you prefer to maintain a 70/30 or 80/20 mix from the very beginning, then add to the bond fund as part of your ongoing investment allocation throughout your primary investing years. Keep in mind if you downsize your home once you retire, any extra equity from the sale can make for a nice "surge" investment into your bond fund.

Avoid Chasing Returns

It's tempting to shoot for big returns, especially as a beginning investor. You want to score big and make a lot of money, so sometimes, unfortunately, your first investments turn out to be among your worst. Certainly that was the case for us. Instead of buying meat-and-potatoes index funds, which seemed frankly boring to us at the time, we chased the potentially higher returns offered by actively managed and specialty funds.

The Lure of Top 100 Lists

As novice investors we scoured the financial magazines for the "best of the best" mutual funds. Top 100 lists that ranked funds based on their recent performance were a particular draw. Perhaps it isn't too surprising therefore that we found ourselves avidly tracking the best funds on these lists and making our initial selections from the ones at or near the top. Whatever fund had performed the best over the past five or ten years was the one we wanted to invest in next. Well-placed ads for the self-same mutual funds tended to underscore the wisdom of investing in these funds above all others.

They say past performance is no guarantee of future results, and it turns out they mean it. The problem with chasing returns is that you end up buying high and selling low – the exact opposite of what you want to do. Funds with outsized returns have often had to take outsized risks in order to get where they are at the top of the leaderboard. They rarely stay there for long. The big bets that got them there in the first place often sink them once markets shift or investor sentiment changes. Expense ratios can also be dramatically higher for these high-flying funds, and that tends to pull them back down to earth over the long run.

Our first taxable investment is a good case in point. In 1994 we put $2,000 into an overseas emerging markets fund right at the tail-end of an amazing five-year run for emerging markets stocks. It was hardly surprising such funds were at the pinnacle of *all* mutual funds at that point, right at the top of the Top 100 lists. Predictably enough, given its high valuation and its high fees, the fund performed substantially below par after we bought it. We eventually had to sell it for a slight loss some six or seven years later when we finally made the switch to index fund investing.

Our second taxable investment was equally questionable, a momentum growth fund riding high in the #1 position on the leaderboard when we bought it. The fund fully embraced the concept of momentum investing – that is, buying a growth stock when it is on a tear and riding it up even higher. This was a very mid-1990's investment to make. We were right in the midst of the dot-com boom and it seemed like technology stocks could never go down again. The fund really did go on a tear at first, then the momentum fizzled before going the wrong way fast. We got out in time to avoid the worst of the carnage, but once again we found ourselves disappointed with a fund we had felt very excited about at first.

High Valuations, High Risks, High Expenses

It took two or three setbacks like this before we learned our lesson the hard way. Buying actively managed funds with high valuations, high risks, and high expenses in the hopes of scoring big did not make a whole lot of sense. Nor did it make sense for us as beginning investors to be buying funds with such a narrow focus – such as emerging markets or momentum growth funds. Instead we should have been concentrating our efforts on building a healthy core portfolio. In other words, we should have been buying highly diversified stock index funds with low fees.

It took us a long time to learn this lesson, and we hope you can learn from our mistakes and make a healthier start to your investing program than we did. If you want to buy niche market funds, at least wait to do it until after you have a healthy core portfolio built up. Sector and specialty funds should be considered dessert, not the main course.

Steadily buying low-cost index funds may not be the most glamorous thing in the world, but ask yourself why you are investing in the first place. Is it for the rush that comes from making a big return? Or is it for the reward of reaching your retirement goal successfully? The rush to score big has more to do with gambling than investing, whereas a buy-and-hold approach to index fund investing is one you can use throughout your life as a reliable strategy for getting rich slowly.

Other Options Besides Mutual Funds

Mutual funds aren't the only game in town: there are other viable options for getting rich slowly through a program of steady investments. We'd like to touch briefly on a few of these.

Exchange Traded Funds

Exchange Traded Funds, or ETFs, are close cousins of mutual funds. They tend to be low-cost and tax-efficient and they trade like a stock. Whereas mutual funds are bought or sold at the end of each trading day, ETFs trade throughout the day at prices that can be higher or lower than their net asset value. There is no minimum investment requirement for ETFs – a key benefit to beginning investors – and you can invest as much or as little money as you wish.

ETFs also offer tax benefits to investors. Mutual funds must distribute capital gains to their shareholders on a yearly basis (i.e., whenever shares have been sold at a profit in order to keep the portfolio in line with the weighted index being tracked). These gains are taxable even if you reinvest the distributions in more shares of the same fund. By comparison, investors in ETFs generally only realize capital gains when they sell shares. This gives them a bit more control over when they realize capital gains and have to pay taxes on them.

Most ETFs track an index and are thus highly diversified. They can hold stocks, bonds, and even commodities. Their expense ratios tend to be lower than those for comparable mutual funds. One reason for this is that an ETF does not have to maintain a cash reserve for redemptions. The Vanguard S&P 500 ETF (VOO), for example, has an ultra-low 0.05% expense ratio. That matches the expense ratio for the "Admiral Shares" version of its Index 500 fund and is lower than the "Investor Shares" version.

Brokerage commissions sometimes apply when you are buying or selling an ETF. An important exception is typically made, however, when you are buying or selling ETFs offered by your own investment firm. For example, Vanguard ETFs can be bought and sold commission-free through Vanguard Brokerage Services. To discourage day trading, Vanguard allows 25 free trades of the same ETF in a 12-month period before restricting further trading for 60 days.

A diversified ETF index fund held over the long term can be a solid investment choice, but the very ability of an ETF to trade like a stock can sometimes be a downside in that it increases the temptation to engage in market timing or short-term speculation.

Still, there is a lot to like about ETFs and not much to dislike. We can certainly see the virtues of investing in them. Perhaps out of a sense of familiarity if nothing else, we have remained dedicated mutual fund investors. We believe mutual funds and ETFs offer roughly comparable experiences as long as you are already investing with a low-cost investment firm like Vanguard.

Individual Value Stocks

Individual stocks offer another worthy alternative to mutual funds or ETFs. If you decide to go this route, be sure to give yourself a basic education in financial matters first so you have the groundwork needed to be an astute investor. We recommend you read a book or two about Warren Buffett, widely considered the most successful investor of the 20th century, to get an idea of his value approach to investing.

Buffett's advice at its most basic is to purchase businesses at a large discount to their intrinsic value, which means avoiding high-flying growth stocks and sticking instead to companies that are undervalued by the market for one reason or another.

These companies may be temporarily on the ropes but are likely to make a strong comeback.

If you can learn to be a contrarian investor and buy stocks when they're beaten down but fundamentally sound, you'll have gone a long way towards becoming a wise investor. It's easy to be lured by tech companies making sexy products, but these same stocks are frequently overpriced because too many other people want them too, and usually for the wrong reasons. By comparison, what might look like a boring old value stock at first glance can pack a lot of punch. Instead of focusing on what a company *does*, we recommend you focus on what it *returns*. Let that be the determining factor in whether you deem a company to be exciting or not.

Bear markets can be a smart investor's best friend. Keep an eye out for stocks that have been battered along with the market as a whole even though their fundamentals are sound. You can also look for companies that have been beaten up in the news recently but are intrinsically sound. Netflix comes to mind as a recent example. A series of managerial missteps sent the stock sharply downward, yet the underlying business model was sound and the company continued to earn profits. An astute investor might have stepped in and purchased shares when they were at or near their lows and reaped the rewards later on.

Sometimes an opportunity comes along that isn't available to the general public. As an employee at my aerospace firm, for example, I was able to take advantage of my company's employee stock purchase plan. It allowed me to purchase shares of their stock which the company matched 20% up to certain monthly dollar limits. That's quite a deal when you think about it: it's like getting a 20% free return on your investment even if the underlying stock price remains flat. Once we had wrapped our minds around that idea, we bought a fair amount of company stock over the years. Not surprisingly it turned out to be one of our best investments, especially when the stock price itself started to rise appreciably. Keep an eye out for similar opportunities in your own life, especially with regard to the company for which you work.

The major downside to investing in individual stocks is that your risk is higher because you're invested in only a handful of stocks at a time. You're much less diversified than you would be with an index fund, and if one or two of your stocks should plummet, it could have a big impact on your portfolio. On the other hand, if you're a shrewd investor and your stocks perform well, you stand to benefit in a big way.

Unfortunately most of us aren't as astute at stock picking as Warren Buffett, so unless you are particularly confident of your abilities in this regard, we would recommend you stick to index fund investing as the safer and more reliable approach. However, if we were to do it all over again, we would at least consider value stock investing as a worthy alternative solution to achieving financial independence. Some combination of index fund investing and value stock investing is also worth considering.

Any Other Options?

We'll briefly mention two other options that come to mind for reaching your early retirement goals.

Buying and selling real estate offers a feasible approach to achieving financial independence, provided you have a good understanding of your local real estate market and a sharp eye for value. In some cases this might involve flipping homes, where you put sweat equity into a fixer-upper then resell it at a profit, and in others it might involve establishing a collection of rental properties in your local area that you manage and rent out on a monthly basis. We don't presume to give advice on this subject since it was not the approach we took. We merely mention it because we know of others who have taken this tack to creating a monthly income stream and it worked for them. We suspect it would demand more hands-on effort, though, and might require you to be physically present to manage the business after you retired.

Another option worth mentioning is becoming an entrepreneur and starting your own business. Of course the sky is the limit with this approach: you could not only get rich slowly but get rich quick if you hit upon the right business opportunity. On the other hand, the risk of being an entrepreneur can be quite high so it takes courage to choose this option. In effect all your eggs are in one basket – your business – so if it fails your dream of early retirement can fail along with it, or at least be sidetracked for a time. But if it succeeds it could offer substantial financial well-being and a genuine sense of accomplishment.

Not long ago we met a couple named Steve and Lynn Miller (webetripping.com) who successfully took the entrepreneurial approach to financial independence. They started a software business in 1998 with a $10,000 investment of their own money and maintained 100% ownership of the business until they sold it in 2009. Early retirement was a part of their plan from the very beginning. They achieved their goal and retired at ages 50 and 52 – while raising two kids no less. We met up with them just as they were dropping their kids off to college and venturing off on a three-month trip to Ecuador, Peru, and the Bahamas. We were impressed by the guts it took for them to start their own business, manage cash flow issues, work long hours, and eventually sell their software business for a healthy profit.

For those who have the ingenuity and temperament for it, the entrepreneurial path can be a satisfying and rewarding one. For the rest of us, a reliable job and some simple index fund investing may be the preferable route. Slow and steady wins the race for most of us and offers what may be the safest path to early retirement.

Chapter 12.
Take Advantage of 401(k)s and IRAs

I remember reading for the first time as a beginning investor about the advantages of investing in a 401(k) plan and feeling energized about saving for the future in a way I never had before. The triple benefit of a company match, tax-deferred growth, and lower taxes was simply too good to pass up. I got started right away investing in the 401(k) plan offered through my company. It felt like we were being handed the keys to a shiny new car that could speed us faster towards our goal. Not only did it let us cut through the headwinds of taxes with less effort, it also incentivized us to do what we wanted to do anyway: save for the future.

About halfway through our investing years, a new kind of individual retirement account became available called a Roth IRA, and once again it felt like we were being handed a surprisingly generous gift. This one offered unlimited potential for earnings to compound without being taxed – ever! That seemed almost too magnanimous on the government's part – but it didn't stop us from taking full advantage of it.

Benefits of Tax-Advantaged Accounts

Tax-advantaged accounts offer a carrot in the form of tax breaks to those who are willing to put aside a portion of their money today to prepare for their own future tomorrow. In this chapter we focus primarily on two types of tax-advantaged accounts, 401(k)s and Roth IRAs. Both offer distinct advantages, which is why we recommend you don't limit yourself to one but invest in both types.

Tax Sheltering

Sheltering your retirement money from taxes is a genuine comfort come tax season. It's as if this money were invisible to the IRS (but in a completely legal way, of course). As long as you don't withdraw it before age 59½, you don't even have to think about it at tax time. But with taxable accounts you *do* have to think about it, because certain investments – mutual funds and bonds among them – generate dividends and capital gains that you have to pay taxes on even if those dividends and capital gains are reinvested. Taxable accounts are a pay-as-you-go system, whereas tax-advantaged accounts let you shelter a portion of your money from Uncle Sam until a much later date, which is definitely to your advantage.

Faster Compounding

You'll often hear it said that 401(k)s and traditional IRAs let your investments compound faster than they would in a taxable account. This is true after a fashion but requires some explanation. If you invest exactly the same dollar amounts in exactly the same investments in a taxable and a tax-advantaged account, they will compound at exactly the same rate. But it is usually assumed you are contributing more dollars to a tax-advantaged account than you are to a taxable one. Why? Because it's easier to invest pre-tax dollars than it is to invest after-tax dollars.

Think about it this way: investing $10,000 pre-tax is roughly the equivalent of investing $7,500 after-tax (assuming you are in a 25% tax bracket). It takes no extra effort on your part to get the $2,500 "bonus" by investing pre-tax dollars in a tax-advantaged account. Thus it is fair in a sense to compare investing $10,000 in pre-tax dollars to $7,500 in after-tax dollars. With this assumption understood, then it becomes clear why a 401(k) or a traditional IRA compounds faster than a taxable account: because $10,000 really does compound faster than $7,500.

Of course not all tax-advantaged accounts are the same these days. With a Roth IRA you invest after-tax dollars, so the faster compounding assumption doesn't apply to your contribution amounts. It could be argued earnings compound faster since no taxes are owed on reinvested dividends and capital gains, but this is a fairly hollow distinction. Why? Because taxes are usually paid out of your *current* income stream, not out of your investments themselves. Thus paying taxes on reinvested dividends and capital gains in a taxable account may make your pocketbook lighter, but it does not generally inhibit the compounding of the investments themselves.

Easy Rebalancing

Tax-advantaged accounts let you rebalance funds and transfer assets within the same account with no tax consequences. By comparison, every time you transfer dollars to rebalance your portfolio in a taxable account, it results in a taxable event for the year.

We rebalance our taxable portfolio after a fashion by withdrawing money for living expenses from whatever fund has performed best of late. However, we rarely move money from one fund to another because of the tax consequences of doing so. By comparison, it's a breeze to move money around in a tax-advantaged account because there *are* no tax consequences. This considerably increases your flexibility to make adjustments and fine-tune your portfolio through the years.

One Disadvantage: Limitations on Access

For early retirees, the biggest challenge of investing in tax-advantaged accounts is the limitation on accessing your money before age 59½. Withdrawing money before that point typically results in having to pay a steep 10% penalty tax on top of the ordinary income taxes owed. This limitation is especially significant for those retiring extra-early in their thirties or forties. The next section discusses strategies you can employ to address these concerns.

Allocating Between Taxable and Tax-Advantaged Accounts

The preferred order of investing for a typical retirement is usually summarized as follows:

1. Invest enough in your 401(k) to receive the maximum possible match
2. Invest the maximum yearly amount in your Roth IRA(s)
3. Invest more in your 401(k) up to your yearly contribution limit
4. Invest any additional amount in your taxable account

This rule of thumb makes perfectly good sense if you plan to retire at age 55 or older. However, if you plan to retire very early – say, in your thirties or forties – then you need to give the matter some additional consideration. You're going to require funds you can access without limitation or penalty before age 59½. In a sense you're going to need to save for *two* retirements – the near-term one and the post-age-59½ one.

Since it isn't the norm to retire in your thirties or forties, you rarely see this issue addressed in the financial media. Nevertheless it is a very real one for anyone hoping to retire well before the age of 59½.

Taxable Accounts and the Ultra-Early Retiree

The simplest option if you are planning a very early retirement is to invest more in your taxable account. This gives you complete freedom to access your money however and whenever you like. There are no penalties, no age limits, and no regulatory or bureaucratic hoops to jump through. That's the beauty of a taxable account: the money is yours and you can do with it as you wish.

The main downside of this approach is that the burden of taxes can be heavy during your final working years when you not only have a high salary but may also have large amounts of taxable investments throwing off dividends and capital gains as you prepare for your imminent retirement. You may want to voluntarily increase your withholding amounts during these years to account for the higher taxes you're likely to experience. However, the instant you retire from the workforce, this burden is lifted and your taxes drop dramatically.

When we first started dreaming about early retirement, we contemplated leaving the work force at age 55. With that retirement age in mind, it made sense for most of our money to be invested in my 401(k) plan at work and in our Roth IRAs. We figured a small taxable account would be all we would need to cover us for the 4½ years or so until age 59½. However, as we began making detailed plans, we kept pushing our target retirement age earlier, first to age 50, then to age 45, and in the end to age 43.

About halfway through our primary saving years, we realized we were woefully underfunded for the first 15 years of our retirement before age 59½. As a result we dramatically increased the percentage of our investment dollars going into our taxable account, realizing we would need those dollars to cover us for a longer period of time than we had originally anticipated.

In the end we overshot a bit and saved more in our taxable account than we did in our tax-advantaged accounts. At retirement we held almost $350,000 in taxable investments as compared to $280,000 in tax-advantaged investments (a 55/45 split). We think a 50/50 split (not including the equity in our home) would have been closer to ideal.

Our total taxable account at retirement stood at nearly $550,000. (This includes $200,000 in bond funds from the sale of our home but excludes $100,000 set aside for future home-buying purposes.) This amount generated enough capital gains, interest, and dividends to provide us with a decent source of income during our early retirement years. The withdrawals we made were replenished for the most part by our taxable investment earnings.

Not surprisingly, our taxable account has slowly diminished over the past six years while our untapped 401(k) and Roth IRA investments have continued to grow. Compare the year-end totals in 2006 (when we retired) to the year-end totals in 2012:

Account	2006	2012	Difference
Taxable	$547,540	$506,064	-$41,476
Tax-Advantaged	$278,679	$320,567	+41,888
	$826,219	$826,631	+$412

You can see the totals for both years are almost identical, but the allocation of investments has shifted towards more money in our 401(k) and Roth IRAs and less in our taxable account. This is in line with our overall expectations, in which we envision our taxable account staying even or slowly diminishing while our 401(k) and Roth IRA accounts continue to grow until age 59½. At that point we can tap into those funds as well without penalty. This strategy has worked well for us overall, and we would recommend it to others as a viable approach to ultra-early retirement.

Keep in mind the above results encompass the Great Recession and its aftermath, a difficult period by anyone's reckoning. Breaking even is probably about the best we could have hoped for during this challenging time, but it seems reasonable to hope for better results in the years to come.

Tax-Advantaged Accounts and the Ultra-Early Retiree

We find it something of a comfort to have a substantial portion of our investments continuing to grow untouched in our 401(k) and Roth IRAs. We feel like we still have a retirement fund off to the side that's meant for the long term, even while we tap into the taxable account for our shorter-term needs.

Our hope, of course, is that our overall investment portfolio will continue to grow thanks to our 401(k) and Roth IRA investments. That should allow us to withdraw more money in future years, which in turn will allow us to keep up with inflation and maintain a standard of living similar to or better than the one we enjoy today. Only time and market conditions will tell if our expectations are to be realized or not, but we continue to believe we're on the right track.

Another Good Option for Retirees Age 55 and Over

For those retiring at or around the age of 55, there is another good option to consider: relying on the direct contributions you've made over the years to your Roth IRA.

You're always allowed to withdraw your own contributions tax- and penalty-free from a Roth IRA (but not the earnings). Whether those contributions will be enough to cover you until the rest of your tax-advantaged funds kick in at age 59½ is food for careful thought. But if you like the idea of investing solely in tax-advantaged accounts, this gives you a promising strategy to pursue.

To determine if this is feasible for you, add up how much of your Roth IRA account is likely to consist of your own contributions by the time you reach your target retirement age. For example, let's say you and your spouse are age 30 and each of you has started investing the current maximum of $5,500 per year in a Roth IRA account. You hope to retire by age 55. That gives you 25 years x $11,000 per year = $275,000 of contributions to your Roth IRAs (or possibly more than that, assuming contribution limits go up in the future).

You'll need to cover about five years of early retirement until age 59½, so that works out to $275,000 ÷ 5 = $55,000 of income per year. That's not too bad. Over the course of those five years you may deplete most of the contributions from your account, but your earnings will continue to grow.

Relying on Roth contributions alone becomes less feasible the earlier you decide to retire. For instance, if you were to retire at age 50 instead of 55 in the example above, that would give you 20 years instead of 25 in which to save, resulting in 20 years x $11,000 per year = $220,000 of contributions, which would need to last for roughly 10 years instead of 5. That works out to just $22,000 of income per year until age 59½, which is probably insufficient in and of itself. However, if you planned to supplement this amount with income from a taxable account or a part-time job, then it would become more feasible.

Other Ways to Access Your Money Early

Other strategies for accessing your money early are less attractive because they tend to be more complicated. For example, under certain circumstances it is possible to make withdrawals from your 401(k) account penalty-free after age 55. But for this to work, you have to be sure to terminate your employment no earlier than age 55. If you stop working at age 54¾, then penalties for early withdrawal would still apply. Your 401(k) also has to be with your current company, not with a company you worked for earlier in your career, so you would want to be sure to always roll over your 401(k) to each new employer with whom you take a job.

Now let's say you turn 55 and it's time to take the money out of your 401(k). You *may* be offered the choice to do it in the form of periodic withdrawals. Since a lump sum withdrawal would rocket you into the highest possible tax bracket for the year, periodic withdrawals are the smart way to go. However, many companies don't want the hassle of managing periodic withdrawals, so you may not be given this option. In that case, assuming you don't want to pay taxes on the entire lump sum amount, you would need to roll it over into a traditional IRA. At that point the age 59½ limit would once again apply. But read on, there's a way around that too.

The loophole for traditional or rollover IRAs is this: you can withdraw money penalty-free before age 59½ *if* you take the money out in what the IRS calls "substantially equal periodic payments" (SEPP). This involves annually withdrawing a fixed sum of money from your IRA as determined by an IRS formula that takes into consideration your life expectancy among other factors.

You would have to continue making SEPP withdrawals for at least five years or until you reach age 59½, whichever is *longer*. That means if you retire at age 50, you would need to continue withdrawing SEPPs for 9½ years until you turned 59½. If you were 58 you'd have to take them until you were age 63 since the 5-year minimum would apply. Otherwise you'll get hit with the 10% penalty and *retroactive* interest charges.

Honestly, we find all this a bit too intimidating, and so we decided long ago not to take this route. It seemed to us like the potential for bureaucratic and tax headaches was simply too high. However, it does offer another viable approach to tapping into your 401(k) and traditional IRA money sooner than you could otherwise with no penalty.

In a Nutshell

Only you can decide on the exact percentages that are right for you, but here are our general recommendations regarding allocations between taxable and tax-advantaged accounts:

- If you plan to retire in your thirties or forties, invest 50% of your money in tax-advantaged accounts and 50% in a taxable account.

- If you plan to retire in your early fifties, allocate 75% to tax-advantaged accounts and 25% to a taxable account.

- If you plan to retire in your mid to late fifties or beyond, allocate 100% to tax-advantaged accounts, with any overflow going into a taxable account.

If you feel you already know all you need to know about 401(k)s and IRAs, feel free to skip ahead to the next chapter. Otherwise, read on. We provide a quick overview of each major type of tax-advantaged account: 401(k), Roth IRA, and Traditional IRA. We also make brief mention of educational savings accounts.

401(k) Plans

Nearly every investor the world over will agree on one thing: never turn down free money. That's why nearly every book or article you'll ever read on retirement will urge you to contribute at least enough to your employer-sponsored 401(k) plan to get the full company match. In fact, contributing enough to get the maximum match is the very first thing you should do as an investor.

The 401(k) Company Match

Matches differ from one company to the next. Some companies offer no match at all. Others match their employees' contributions at fifty cents to the dollar up to a specified percentage of pay (commonly 6%). Others are even more generous and match dollar for dollar. But any match is an offer of free money just for participating in a plan that is good for you anyway. It's such a no-brainer that many companies automatically enroll you in their 401(k) plans, requiring you to opt out if you *don't* want to participate.

Let's say you're earning $80,000 gross and your company matches fifty cents to the dollar up to 6% of pay. Your maximum match would be calculated as follows: $80,000 x 6% = $4,800 x $0.50 = $2,400. *You* would need to contribute $4,800 (6% of your gross pay) to receive the maximum company match of $2,400 per year. That's $7,200 altogether, making a nice dent in your investment goals for the year.

Tax-Deferred Growth

Any money you invest in your 401(k) comes straight out of your gross paycheck and grows tax-deferred. Using pre-tax money to fund tax-deferred growth is a very nice deal indeed. Suppose you earn $100,000 gross per year and put 10% of your paycheck into your 401(k). That's 10% of your gross salary, not your net. That means you're investing $10,000, not $7,500 as would otherwise be the case after taxes. This larger tax-deferred amount compounds more quickly than a smaller amount would, giving you a leg up on reaching your retirement goals sooner. The dividends, interest, and capital gains inside your 401(k) account also grow tax-deferred.

Reduced Income Taxes

Matching funds plus tax-deferred growth is a pretty powerful combination in its own right, but what makes it even more potent is this: you actually lower your federal income taxes in the current year by investing in a 401(k) plan. In the example above, it's as if you effectively erased $10,000 off the top of your salary as far as the IRS is concerned and only earned $90,000 instead of $100,000. You would have had to pay about $2,500 in taxes on that extra $10,000, but instead that tax payment is deferred into the far distant future.

Of course you'll have to pay taxes on that money eventually when you withdraw it in retirement, but by then you'll undoubtedly be in a lower tax bracket than you are now. At present you're earning a healthy salary and paying taxes like there's no tomorrow, in part because you're paying taxes on *all* your income but only using a portion of it to live on (with the rest being invested). But when you retire you'll be living a financially simpler life, and your tax bill will reflect that. Thus it makes sense to invest as much as possible in your 401(k) to reduce your current tax load.

Raising Your Percentage

Whenever you get a raise, it's a great time to revisit your 401(k) percentages. Since you haven't become used to living on the higher amount yet, you can take all or a portion of the pay increase off the table and put it into your 401(k) instead. You can be "pretend poor" and convince yourself you still have to make do on roughly the same amount as you did before the raise. This is a powerful way to increase your savings for the future. If you never see the money in your checkbook account, it's almost as if it never existed. But when you look at your 401(k) statement at the end of the year, you'll realize all those extra dollars are making a big difference to your bottom line.

If you increase your percentages incrementally and time them to coincide with pay raises, you may not notice that much of a difference in terms of your take-home pay. Since your 401(k) deductions lower your gross salary, the taxes being withheld from your paycheck are also comparably less, so the overall effect on your take-home pay is often smaller than you might expect.

Investing for Long-Term Capital Appreciation

Most 401(k) plans offer a wide range of mutual fund options. We recommend you do your most aggressive investing in tax-advantaged accounts like your 401(k) and IRA since you won't be touching this money for a long time to come. Compounding can work its greatest magic if you invest in assets such as stock-based mutual funds that have a strong potential for long-term capital appreciation.

One caution: many companies allow you to purchase shares of company stock within your 401(k), and while you may want to invest some money in such a fashion, we suggest you don't go overboard. It's risky to put all your retirement eggs in one basket in case your company should turn out to be (heaven forbid) the next Enron.

Set It and Forget It

Once you've made your selections, you're done for the year. You don't have to revisit your 401(k) plan or make any other decisions until next year's benefits review, when you should reevaluate your percentages and investment selections to make sure they're still right for you. Meanwhile, automatic deductions from your regular paycheck allow you to simply "set it and forget it."

Contribution Limits and Vesting

The IRS sets limits on how much you can contribute to your 401(k) plan in any given year. The limit for 2013 is $17,500; this limit may rise in the future based on cost of living increases. Your company may also impose a maximum percentage salary limit such as 15% of salary. Some plans allow for catch-up contributions, with higher limits for people age 50 and older.

Many 401(k) plans make you wait before you become fully vested in matching funds. This is designed to incentivize you to remain employed with the company for longer than just a year or two. You are always 100% vested in money you contribute directly, but a company may, for instance, give you 25% vesting of matching funds after your first year of employment, 50% after the second year, 75% after the third year, and 100% after the fourth year and beyond.

401(k) Portability

If you leave your job, you can either keep your 401(k) funds in place or take them with you. Taking them with you entails rolling your 401(k) money over, with its tax-deferred status intact, to your new employer's plan. Alternatively, you can roll it over into a traditional IRA set up with an account provider of your choice, such as Vanguard or Fidelity. This is worth considering, especially if your new company's plan is limited in terms of its investment choices. The one thing you should *not* do under any circumstances is cash out the proceeds from your 401(k) plan when you leave your job. Besides having to pay taxes at ordinary tax rates plus a 10% penalty fee, you lose out on potentially decades worth of tax-deferred compounding.

Penalties for Early Withdrawal

The rules are quite strict with regard to early withdrawals from a 401(k). Almost any withdrawals before age 59½ will result in your having to pay taxes at ordinary tax rates plus a 10% penalty fee – giving you a strong inducement to leave your 401(k) money in place once it's there. Even so-called hardship withdrawals (i.e., to cover the downpayment on a first home) are subject to these taxes and penalties.

If you simply must access your 401(k) money because you have no other option, consider taking out a 401(k) loan. We don't recommend this approach except as a last resort, since you are reducing the amount of money that can compound in your account until the loan is repaid, but it's better than taking the money out altogether.

401(k) Taxes in Retirement

All money withdrawn from a 401(k) or a traditional IRA after age 59½ is treated as ordinary income. Even tax-favored capital gains are treated as such. This is one reason we recommend you invest some money in a 401(k) and some in a Roth IRA. That way you can choose how much money to withdraw from each type of account depending on your tax situation in any given retirement year.

You must begin making required minimum distributions from your 401(k) or traditional IRA after you turn age 70½. The amount you need to take out each year is based on IRS life expectancy tables. One benefit of a Roth IRA is that it doesn't have these minimum distribution requirements.

Roth 401(k) Hybrids

A hybrid 401(k) investment called a Roth 401(k) has become popular in recent years and is being offered by more and more companies. It combines some of the best features of both types of investment in that it typically includes a match while also allowing your earnings to grow untaxed forever.

The downside is that you have to invest after-tax dollars instead of pre-tax dollars, so you lose out on some of the tax deferral benefits of a traditional 401(k). Some companies offer both types of 401(k) so you can choose which portion of your retirement plan contributions should go into which type of account.

Roth IRAs

By now you know the main benefit of the Roth IRA is its ability to perpetually shelter your investment earnings from taxation – and that's quite the benefit. When you withdraw money from a Roth IRA after age 59½, you need pay no taxes on it whatsoever. Your contributions were already taxed beforehand, and your earnings escape taxation altogether by virtue of the Roth's design. Since earnings are perpetually sheltered, a Roth is the perfect place to do some of your most aggressive investing. If you are convinced a particular type of investment will appreciate dramatically over the long term, make that investment in your Roth account.

No Required Minimum Distributions

An important advantage of a Roth is that minimum distribution rules at age 70½ don't apply. That means if you're able to get by on other resources in retirement, you don't have to draw down your Roth as you must a 401(k) or traditional IRA. As a result, your Roth earnings can continue to grow tax-free even through your golden years. This makes the Roth IRA a great savings vehicle for the long term – and when we say long term we mean it, since the assets in a Roth IRA can be passed on to heirs.

Only a surviving spouse can continue to contribute to an inherited Roth IRA or combine it with his or her own. Other beneficiaries can, however, set up distributions over the course of their own lifetimes – and pass on whatever might remain to a secondary beneficiary with the tax-free status still intact.

Withdrawals of Contributions and Earnings

We've already touched on the fact that with a Roth IRA your own direct contributions can always be withdrawn tax-free at any time with no early distribution penalties. Of course you would want to avoid doing so if at all possible during your investing years, since it would run counter to the very reason you invested in the Roth in the first place.

Five tax years must have elapsed since your very first Roth IRA contribution was made before *earnings* are considered qualified and can be distributed tax-free. This holds true even if you are over age 59½. However, the five-year clock does not reset each time you make another contribution to your Roth.

No Effect on Social Security

Any money withdrawn from a Roth IRA is not included in the formula used to determine how much of your social security benefits are taxable. Other sources of income – such as wages, interest, dividends, and pensions – can all result in your having to pay taxes on your social security benefits, but not Roth withdrawals.

Suppose you're earning social security benefits while doing a bit of work on the side. If you're married filing jointly and earned between $32,000 and $44,000 in 2012, then up to 50% of your social security income may be taxable – or up to 85% if you earned over $44,000. However, any amounts withdrawn from your Roth IRA have no tax consequences whatsoever and won't add to your potential tax burden.

First-Time Homebuyer Exception

The usual early withdrawal penalties apply if you withdraw *earnings* from your Roth IRA before age 59½ – with one important exception. You can withdraw up to $10,000 in earnings tax- and penalty-free if you are a first-time homebuyer or have not owned a principal residence for more than two years. (This assumes your Roth account has been in place for more than five years.) If you are a couple with two accounts, you can each withdraw up to $10,000. We aren't recommending you use your Roth in such a fashion, but again, it increases your flexibility.

Roth Contribution and Income Limits

As of 2013 you can contribute up to $5,500 to a Roth IRA (plus an extra $1,000 if you're over age 50). Limits are likely to increase in $500 increments in the future based on inflation. For married couples, each spouse can contribute up to the yearly limit. A working spouse can contribute on behalf of a nonworking spouse.

You can only invest in a Roth IRA if you have earned income from a job. You cannot use unearned income such as interest, dividends, capital gains, rental property income, pensions, or social security benefits. We had initially planned on continuing to fund our Roth IRAs during our early retirement years using proceeds from our taxable account, but we eventually came to realize this was not an option.

If you're a highly paid worker, income limits can affect how much you're allowed to contribute to a Roth IRA or whether you can contribute at all. As of 2013 the upper income limit to qualify for a *full* contribution is $112,000 for single filers and $178,000 for joint filers. If you're running up against these limits, one way you can reduce your gross income is to make contributions to your 401(k) plan.

Roth Conversions

Converting a traditional IRA or 401(k) to a Roth IRA has significant tax consequences. Since such money has never been taxed, income taxes are owed on the entire conversion amount. The tax bill for such a conversion should ideally be paid not out of the 401(k) or IRA itself, but rather out of non-IRA funds to avoid reducing your invested amount (and to avoid paying a 10% penalty on the portion of the money used to pay the tax).

You do not have to convert your entire account in one fell swoop. If you have $100,000 you want to convert to a Roth, for example, you can convert $10,000 each year for ten years, thus spreading your tax bill over a longer time period. There are no income limits for converting to a Roth, which gives high earners who otherwise might not qualify to contribute to a Roth a back door into a Roth.

Setting Up a Roth Account

You can set up a Roth IRA account with any major investment firm (Vanguard, Fidelity, Charles Schwab, etc.). You cannot open a "joint IRA" account; each IRA needs to be opened in the name of an individual person. That means you'll have to set up a separate account for yourself and one for your spouse if you're married. This tends to result in some inevitable duplication of funds within your overall portfolio. While you *could* choose to own different funds within each account, it's usually easiest to have the two accounts mirror one another.

In our own case we actually have four different types of accounts: a Roth IRA in my name, a Roth IRA in Robin's name, a 401(k) in my name, and a joint taxable account in both our names. This just goes to show that even when you try to keep things simple, some complexity is unavoidable when you invest.

Synergy Between 401(k)s and Roth IRAs

We like the synergy that comes from investing in both a 401(k) and a Roth IRA. They are the yin and yang of the investing world. The 401(k) gives you matching funds, tax-deferred growth, and current tax deductions, while the Roth IRA gives you entirely tax-free withdrawals and no minimum required distributions at age 70½. The two work well together and don't interfere with each other the way a 401(k) and a traditional IRA sometimes can, as discussed below.

Traditional IRAs and Other Options

A traditional IRA functions similarly to a 401(k) but without the matching fund aspect. Investment earnings grow tax-deferred, and in most cases you can deduct your contributions from current taxes. Contribution limits in 2013 are $5,500 per individual, plus another $1,000 if you're over age 50. The usual age limit of 59½ applies before you can withdraw money without penalty.

Traditional IRA Restrictions

The reason we're less enthusiastic about traditional IRAs is that they have more restrictions on them both in terms of tax deduction eligibility in the present and withdrawals in the future. For instance, you can generally deduct contributions for tax purposes – but not always. Suppose you and your spouse file jointly and are both covered by a retirement plan at work. If together you earn more than $95,000 (as of 2013), then you cannot fully deduct your traditional IRA contributions. Beyond

$115,000 you cannot deduct them at all. This is the conflict we referred to above when we said a 401(k) and traditional IRA can sometimes interfere with one another.

If only one of you is covered by a retirement plan at work, the limits are higher but they still exist. Your deduction begins to phase out beyond $178,000, and no deduction is allowed beyond $188,000. Your earnings still grow tax-deferred within the IRA account, but you have to pay taxes up front on contribution amounts, which eliminates one of the incentives for investing in a traditional IRA in the first place.

Traditional IRAs also require you to begin making required minimum distributions at age 70½. If you don't make them, you automatically lose 50% of the mandatory yearly amount to the IRS.

When Traditional IRAs Still Make Sense

Traditional IRAs are still worth considering under certain circumstances. If your current tax bracket is very high, for instance, and you expect to be in a much lower tax bracket once you retire, there might be good cause to consider investing in a traditional IRA in order to lower your current income taxes. Also, if neither you nor your spouse are covered by a retirement plan at work, or you clearly won't be bumping up against the income limits any time soon, then traditional IRAs become more attractive. At some point, decisions about how best to allocate your money come down to weighing the specifics of your own personal tax situation.

Other Employment-Specific Accounts

While we won't go into detail here, there are other kinds of tax-advantaged accounts that focus on specific employment situations.

- 403(b) plans offer public school teachers and non-profit employees essentially the same benefits as 401(k) plans in the private sector.
- SEP IRAs benefit the self-employed, particularly business owners without employees. They offer tax-deferred growth and very high contribution limits ($51,000 in 2013) which are 100% tax deductible.

- SIMPLE IRAs let small business owners set up low-cost, easy-to-manage retirement plans for their employees that include matching funds and tax-deferred growth.
- Thrift Savings Plans (TSPs) are 401(k)-like plans for federal employees and members of the military.

Tax-Advantaged Educational Accounts

Many parents face the unenviable task of saving at the same time for both their own retirement and their children's higher education. Tax-advantaged educational accounts make the task a little easier. Perhaps the most popular type of account is a 529 plan, which can be used to cover tuition, room and board, and other expenses at accredited institutions. Money can be withdrawn tax-free from these accounts to pay for qualified educational expenses. Student loans and student loan interest are not covered. If a distribution isn't for a qualified educational expense, then the usual income tax and 10% penalty apply.

Each state administers its own 529 plans, and while you can invest in one from out of state, it's usually best to select one from your own state so you can qualify for state income tax deductions and have the potential to receive matching grants and scholarships if they are offered. Since 529 plans are counted as part of *your* assets, they have little impact on your child's eligibility for financial aid within your own state of residence.

Unfortunately you don't get to deduct 529 plan contributions from your federal income taxes, but your money does grow tax-deferred. You maintain control of the account and can even transfer any unused amounts to other qualified members of your family (including yourself and your spouse). You don't make your own investment selections with a 529 plan; instead you enroll in a particular plan which is professionally managed.

Chapter 13.
Live Below Your Means

Mind the gap.

When we visited London for the first time as young adults barely out of college, we stood at Heathrow Airport waiting for the metro to arrive. As it approached and the doors opened, a deep British voice intoned over the loudspeaker, "Mind the gap. Mind the gap." The voice was simply reminding us to watch our step and not fall into the space between the platform and the train as we boarded, but the phrase sounded odd enough to our American ears that it stuck with us. Over time we came to apply it to our financial situation: we learned to mind the gap between making and spending as we saved for the future.

Learning to live below your means is absolutely crucial if you want to retire early and stay retired. To achieve financial independence you need to build capital, and the only way to do that (without help from an outside source) is to make more than you spend. The gap between making and spending has to be big enough that you can put a significant amount of money aside on a monthly basis, year in and year out, for the sole purpose of investing.

One way to increase the make-spend gap is to increase your salary – which is why we suggest you invest in yourself first. The other is to alter your spending habits until you are living well below your means. To achieve financial independence, most people need to tackle the problem from both ends – making more *and* spending less. This two-pronged approach gives you the best chance of widening the gap dramatically enough to make a real difference.

We've already discussed the importance of investing in yourself first, so let's move on to the other side of the equation, spending less.

Tracking Your Expenses

The best way to reduce spending is to become a conscious consumer. Consider the price, look at it twice, and decide if it's really worth it to you given how hard you have to work for your money. Make this one simple adjustment – become conscious of each dollar you spend – and it can make a world of difference in helping you reach your early retirement goals.

Consumer Boot Camp

The most effective way we know to become a more conscious consumer is to put yourself through the equivalent of consumer boot camp and carefully track your expenses down to the penny for a period of time.

We tracked our expenses down to the penny for one whole year and found it burdensome, to be honest, but also enlightening. We would suggest you track your expenses for a period of three months. The exercise will make you focus like never before on where your money is going. The results may surprise you, and you may well come away with a clearer understanding of where you need to cut spending the most.

During boot camp your aim is to look for patterns in spending. Such patterns are easiest to identify if you categorize the information you've collected at the end of each month. We suggest you group your expenses into the following main categories: food, shelter, utilities, clothing, transportation, health, recreation, and miscellaneous. Under each category you can create subcategories as needed. For example, under food you might have subcategories for groceries, dining out, and takeout. Let your own spending habits dictate your subcategories.

Your overall goal is to identify blind spots in your spending habits where cuts can be made. For example, you might discover you're spending much more than you realized on dining out, or on clothing, or on some form of entertainment, or on fancy coffee drinks for that matter. If you find yourself saying, "I never knew I spent *that* much on such-and-such," you've identified a blind spot where you might be able to make some cuts.

During our own boot camp experience, we had several "aha" moments in the first few months. We made cuts in those areas, but after that we couldn't find anywhere else obvious to reduce spending. We had trimmed away most of the fat by then. Wanting to finish what we had started, we continued with the exercise for the rest of the year but found it less helpful after that.

In fact, the exercise eventually became counterproductive for us. Our spending habits actually became too constrained, if such a thing is possible. Since we're already frugal by nature, we really didn't need any extra encouragement to cut back on spending even more. If you're on the frugal side too, remember it's important to keep a sense of balance. Saving up for early retirement demands self-discipline, certainly, but it should not demand self-denial to the point where you feel like you're missing out on things.

In the end, how long you continue the exercise of tracking your expenditures depends on your own personality. Some people keep a budget for life and swear by it, while others do it for a period of time then decide to move on. If you spend money freely, or if you frequently find yourself wondering where it has all gone, you may want to continue tracking your expenses for a longer period of time.

The book *Your Money or Your Life* by Vicki Robin and Joe Dominguez is one we would recommend for its description of how to become a conscious consumer, track your expenses, and rein in spending. The authors clearly describe how to track expenses down to the penny and develop a monthly budget based on the information you collect. The book introduces a concept that was new to us: that money is something we trade our "life energy" for, so we should make certain we are getting a fair trade for it.

Tracking and Budgeting Software

Tracking and categorizing expenses by hand can be laborious, so you may want to use a software program to simplify the process. Personal finance websites like Mint (mint.com) are free to use and make it easy to manage your money online. Mint comes recommended by *Money Magazine* and *The New York Times,* which dubs it "your financial situation in the palm of your hand."

The first step to using Mint is also the most intimidating: you have to add your bank, credit card, home loan, and investment accounts to the website so Mint can securely pull in the information and organize it for you. From that point forward you can see all your accounts in one place, anywhere and any time, including on your mobile phone. Mint uses bank-level security, so if you can get past the concerns of hackers, then there are a lot of benefits to using an online program like this that can link all your financial accounts together and give you the big picture in real time. If you're uncomfortable with the online option, you can use a similar stand-alone program like Quicken.

Both Mint and Quicken let you organize all your accounts in one place, track your spending, and create a personalized budget. They use simple pie charts and graphs to show you where your money is being spent each month. Expenses are automatically categorized – so you can keep track not only of how much you're spending but where. Programs like these take a lot of the hassle out of tracking and budgeting and are definitely worth a look.

Living Simply

There is an attraction to not over-buying, to not overdoing things, to keeping things simple. Being unencumbered by too many possessions can actually be a relief both for the pocketbook and for the mind. Spending less doesn't have to equate with being less happy – in fact, it can be just the opposite.

Living simply means adopting a new mindset. It means letting go of concerns about keeping up with the Joneses and focusing instead on your own well-being, financial and otherwise. As you become more motivated about achieving financial independence, you'll leave old ways of thinking behind and adopt new ones that are more suited to achieving your goal.

Doing what so many others are doing – namely, spending till they're deep in debt or barely breaking even – will never get you where you want to go, so why not take a different tack? Learn to think outside the box when it comes to your own financial well-being. Open your eyes to what life can be like if you live it on your own terms and reject mindless consumerism. More and more people are coming to realize that the endless pursuit of stuff does not make them happy, and in fact clutters the path to happiness.

We're not advocating you live like a monk and never part with a penny, but we do suggest you keep a sense of balance when it comes to spending. Finding that right balance has to do with defining what is genuinely important to you versus what you can do without at minimal sacrifice to yourself.

Kids and Spending

Exercising financial restraint becomes even more challenging when children are involved. It's awfully hard to deny a child something he or she really wants. We want to be generous and deny them nothing. We say to ourselves, "Why should *they* have to go without? It's one thing for me to deny myself something, but who am I to deny them?" It adds a whole new twist to keeping up with the Joneses when it's your kids who are seeing what the Joneses' kids have and want the same.

But you're not doing them any favors if you're teaching them by example that it's okay to overspend and live beyond your means. Frankly, it's not healthy for anyone to live beyond their means for a prolonged period of time. It's stressful and eats away at your sense of happiness and self-esteem. The stress you feel about it inevitably rubs off on your kids too. Wouldn't it be better to teach them by example what it takes to actually live within your means as a family? That a certain amount of sacrifice in pursuit of a long-term goal – whether it be retirement or college education – is a good thing?

By setting an example for your kids and investing for the future, you're teaching them an important life lesson. After all, it won't be long before it's their turn to make a similar journey towards financial independence. That journey will be easier if they have an example to look up to and can say, "My parents did it. If they could do it, so can I."

Retiring Early on Less

Adopting a simpler lifestyle makes it easier to retire early for one simple reason: your nest egg can be smaller. If you learn to live on $40,000 per year, then you only need a nest egg of about $1 million. An income of $80,000 per year will require a nest egg of about $2 million. Of course it takes longer to save $2 million than it does $1 million, so your retirement will necessarily come later than it would have otherwise.

By simplifying your needs, you simplify the whole equation of your life. If your current needs are less, you spend less, which lets you save more. And if your needs in retirement are less, then you don't have to save as much as you would have otherwise. Lessening both your current needs and your future needs makes it easier to balance the make-spend equation of your life and frees you from having to work any longer than you have to.

Where you live is also an important factor in being able to retire early on less. If you reside in an expensive city, you may want to consider moving to a less expensive location once you retire. Otherwise, you'll need to compensate for the higher cost of living where you reside by saving up a larger nest egg. Retiring early on less is much more difficult if the cost of living is double what it would be in a less expensive part of the country.

Reducing Spending

Every day we make a lot of little decisions about how to spend our money, and those decisions add up. When taken together, they play a big role in determining our overall financial health and well-being. Learning to pay attention to the small things that escape most people's notice helps us rein in spending and take control of our personal finances.

Whenever you walk into a store or shop online, it helps to remember you're on the wrong side of the make-spend equation. You're in enemy territory, so to speak. Of course we all need to shop, but there's a difference between shopping out of necessity and shopping for pleasure. Shopping till you drop is a funny expression, but it's also a little depressing when you consider how many people take it literally. It's certainly not a good fit for the aspiring early retiree.

Exercising a little self-restraint should not be considered a bad thing, but nowadays it is sometimes seen as an indication of not valuing yourself highly enough to get what you properly deserve. The words "I deserve it" have become the mantra for those who would justify buying whatever they want without regard for their financial well-being. It's a shame those same words aren't used more often to describe why we should buy less in order to achieve financial independence sooner.

Let's take a look at a few areas of our lives in which we all regularly spend money and consider some strategies that can be employed to reduce spending and keep it under control.

Food, Glorious Food

We admit to being foodies who enjoy a memorable dinner out just as much as the next person. It's one of the great pleasures of life and shouldn't be missed. So we aren't suggesting you go cold turkey and only eat cold turkey! But we are suggesting you limit dining out during your primary investing years to once a week or special occasions.

Let's face it, restaurant dining can be expensive. By the time you figure in the cost of the food, drinks, taxes, and tip, it can take quite a chunk out of your budget, especially if you're dining out multiple times per week. The simplest solution is to limit your number of outings.

When you do dine out, some strategies for keeping costs down might include splitting a generously sized meal, bringing leftovers home for a second meal, or taking advantage of coupon offers and happy hour specials. Ordering takeout can also be a good in-between option. Sometimes we would be hard-pressed to cook a meal for anything less than we pay to split a delicious takeout dinner.

That said, buying your own food at the supermarket and cooking it at home is usually the most economical way to go. It's what we recommend as the norm when you are in "full save mode" and doing everything in your power to keep costs down. The economics become even more compelling if you're a family.

Proven strategies for spending less when you go grocery shopping include clipping coupons, taking advantage of in-store specials, buying in bulk, checking out the bottom shelves where supermarkets tend to put their lowest-priced items, and buying generic instead of brand-name products. Whole books are dedicated to the subject of shopping for groceries economically, so we won't go into further detail here.

Only you can decide if a premium grocery store is worth the extra expense, but we do suggest you make such decisions with at least one eye on cost.

It's also wise to limit impulse purchases at the grocery store. I know of what I speak in this regard. I once came home with a shopping cart's worth of new taste sensations – and a sensationally high receipt to match. I came to realize I'd been thinking of supermarkets as cheap by definition because they didn't involve dining out. But supermarkets can be expensive too, and you can't just shop on auto-pilot with no regard for prices.

You may have similar blind spots in your own spending habits that need to be reined in. If so, identify them and come up with a strategy for dealing with them. My own solution involved learning to shop with a list, limiting myself to one or two items off-list each trip, and shopping when possible on a full stomach.

Clothing and the Joys of Mad Money

If you love to shop for new clothing and know you're spending more on it than you should, try reining in your spending by setting a monthly clothing budget and keeping to it. This may be one area in which you and your partner have differing opinions about what is a sensible amount to spend each month. Sit down together and see if you can come to an agreement about what's reasonable given your overall budget. Your clothing budget and your partner's may differ in amount, but that's okay as long as the total is acceptable to both of you.

One strategy that works well for us is to keep a small stash of personal money to the side. This is our mad money that we can use any way we want without feeling guilty or feeling like we have to justify our purchases to each other. (Not that we really have to, but it's a psychological thing.) Robin uses her personal money to buy "unnecessary" clothing, and I use mine to buy "unnecessary" video games. It's a simple thing that keeps us both happy and doesn't break the bank.

Thankfully you can return impulse clothing purchases if you realize you've gone overboard, but another tack is to walk away from an item if you're unsure about buying it. If it's still on your mind later on, then you know it's something you really want. This gives you time to mull things over before making a purchase. Occasionally you may come to the conclusion the item is too similar to something you already own or is something you wouldn't wear often enough to get your money's worth. This is what being a conscious consumer is all about: thinking about your purchases before making them.

Another strategy is to shop for clothing at secondhand stores. Robin enjoys the treasure hunt aspect of finding clothing she likes at significantly lower prices than she would pay elsewhere. The gently used items at these stores can be of surprisingly good quality. You can also save time and money by sticking with classic looks instead of chasing trends that go in and out of fashion and require frequent replacement.

When it comes to jewelry and accessories, having a few items you treasure – and actually wear – is better than having loads of them cluttering up your jewelry boxes and drawers. For simplicity's sake alone, keeping these purchases to a minimum makes sense.

Entertainment: Proving Ground for Delayed Gratification

Delayed gratification is the ability to wait to obtain something you really want. Of course the biggest form of delayed gratification is retirement itself, where you work hard for a period of years in order to buy time later on without having to work. This same principal applies to many smaller things in life. For instance, if you can bring yourself to wait to see a movie that has just been released, you can see it on DVD or streaming video in just a few months' time at a fraction of the price.

We're not saying you should *always* delay gratification. Sometimes you want to see something on the big screen, and that's that. But you should pick and choose carefully when you know you're spending more on something just for the pleasure of seeing it now. The quality of the movie certainly isn't going to deteriorate in the meantime.

Consider almost any electronic device currently on the market. Wait six months and there's a good chance it will have come down in price, sometimes dramatically. Something newer and better will have come along to replace it. But why should you buy the latest version that has a few extra bells and whistles when, just a few months ago, you would have been perfectly happy with the previous version which is now on sale for much less? Advertisers will try to sell you on the idea that the newest version is the most amazing thing since sliced bread, but you should make your own decision.

Be on the lookout for less expensive ways to do the same thing. Consider buying paperback books at a used bookstore instead of buying them new in hardcover. Visit the library and check out books, audio books, DVDs, CDs, and magazines for free. Read classics in the public domain at no cost on electronic devices. Project Gutenberg (gutenberg.org) offers more than 36,000 free eBooks that can be downloaded onto any portable device or PC.

Keeping yourself entertained can be surprisingly affordable these days. With one laptop or iPhone you can carry weeks' or months' worth of entertainment with you. The truth is, so much free entertainment is available online, you could probably entertain yourself for a lifetime with a simple internet connection and not much else. You can also educate yourself online on just about any subject under the sun at no cost whatsoever.

Recurring Expenses: The Little Things Add Up

We've suggested living below your means requires a new mindset that involves asking yourself on a regular basis if you're getting good value for your money. It means being cognizant of the fact that a lot of seemingly little expenses can add up to a lot over the years. This is especially true when it comes to recurring expenses, which by their very definition are paid month in and month out.

With this in mind, we recommend you take a second look at your phone, internet, cable, and other recurring monthly bills and consider if there are any ways you might reduce spending without causing yourself too much grief. If you're paying for services you rarely use, or for duplicative services (e.g., land lines and mobile services), think about whether there might be a less expensive way to go.

If you rarely use your cell phone, for example, you might consider a prepaid cell phone or a no-contract "pay as you go" phone instead of paying a monthly rate. We found we could save money by having no land line and only carrying a single cell phone with us most of the time. Robin also keeps a backup cell phone (TracFone) for emergencies and occasional use. It offers nationwide coverage with no bills, no contracts, and no daily or monthly fees. Instead, we pay approximately $100 per year for the lowest number of minutes available at the most affordable price.

Another option when it comes to phone service is Skype, which lets you make calls from your computer to other people's phones all around the world for as little as two cents per minute. We use Skype heavily when traveling overseas. We've also come to use it occasionally at home. If we know we're getting close to using up our free "anytime" minutes for a given month on our Verizon cell phone, we switch to using Skype when making lengthy calls during peak periods.

Instead of paying right off the bat for the highest-priced premium internet connection, why not try out the basic option first, then upgrade if you find it's too slow for your needs? This is a better approach than always assuming you need the most expensive service on offer and springing for it without even trying the lower-cost option.

If you're paying for extended cable service and yet rarely venture beyond the major networks, you're not getting good value for your money. Consider basic cable, which can cost as little as $20 per month and may still give you most of the channels you watch. If there's a sporting event you really want to see that isn't available on the basic channels, consider going to your local sports bar and watching it for the price of a beer. Another good option is an indoor digital antenna like the Leaf HDTV Antenna – which might just allow you to get rid of cable and satellite bills altogether.

We're not suggesting you eliminate or downsize services you genuinely use, only the ones you don't use enough to justify the cost. We pay a monthly fee for Netflix, for example, and consider it money well spent since we really do use it. When we're away on vacation overseas, we temporarily put a hold on our Netflix membership so we're not paying for a service we can't use during that period of time.

The good news is, more and more options for different kinds of services are becoming available every day. You don't *have* to go with cable any more simply because there's no other choice. Take advantage of the bounty of options out there, customizing your choices to your lifestyle to get the most bang for your buck.

Chapter 14.
Keep Home and Car Expenses Low

During my early working years I would sometimes daydream about retiring early and living on a yacht in the Caribbean. Now as soon as yachts are involved in your dreams of the future, you know you're in trouble, but in my mind's eye I could see us living half the year in the Caribbean and the other half in the Rockies. I'm reluctant to admit I even have a journal entry where I list my dream goals as follows: 1) to own a log home in the Rockies, 2) to own an island home in the Caribbean, 3) to own an RV for tooling around North America, and 4) to own a small yacht for tooling around the Caribbean.

You'll note the self-restraint involved in only requiring a small yacht to go along with our island home – one of two homes, mind you. I suspect even then I knew I was being a tad unrealistic. I can still envision owning or renting each of these things one at a time, but certainly not all at once.

Fortunately, over time we came to simplify our dreams along with our lives, or otherwise we would have been working well into our old age. We came to realize that simplifying your life goes part and parcel with retiring early on less. And a big part of keeping life simple is keeping two of your biggest expenses in life – home and vehicles – as low as reasonably possible. Making wise decisions in these two areas alone can make a big difference in whether or not you reach your early retirement goals.

Keeping Your Mortgage Affordable

Your home can become one of your best investments or an albatross around your neck, depending on whether you stay within your means or get in too deep. Here's some help in how to tell the difference.

The 28/36 Rule: What Conventional Wisdom Says

Conventional wisdom says your mortgage payment can be up to 28% of your gross income, as long as your total debt payments don't exceed 36% of your income. This is sometimes called the 28/36 rule, and it's what mortgage lenders typically use as a rule of thumb in deciding whether or not you qualify for a loan.

Suppose you and your spouse make $80,000 gross per year. According to the 28/36 rule, your mortgage payment should not exceed $1,867 per month ($80,000 x 28% = $22,400 ÷ 12 = $1,867), and your mortgage payment *plus* any other debts (credit cards, car payments, college loans, etc.) should not exceed $2,400 per month ($80,000 x 36% = $28,800 ÷ 12 = $2,400). Keep in mind these are *not to exceed* amounts. In essence, they are the maximums mortgage lenders want to see in order for you to qualify for a loan.

The 20/28 Rule: A More Conservative Approach

We recommend you keep your housing costs considerably lower than the 28/36 rule allows. Conventional wisdom assumes your goal is to live *within* your means, but since your goal is to live substantially *below* your means, conventional wisdom doesn't necessarily apply.

We recommend 20% of your monthly gross income go toward housing costs instead of 28%. For a couple making $80,000 per year, that would work out to be $1,333 per month in mortgage payments. Ideally you would be debt-free before buying your home, but if that's not feasible, we would suggest you use 28% instead of 36% as a guide for the total amount of debt you should carry. That would be $1,867 per month for our hypothetical couple.

This more conservative 20/28 rule gives you more of a cushion for investing for your future. The last thing you want is to be house poor if you're trying to save for early retirement.

The Downside of Stretching Too Far

Now, some would argue you should stretch as far as conceivably possible to pay for the biggest, nicest home you can afford. They suggest your salary will only grow in the future so the house payments that seem so cumbersome today will become more affordable later on.

While there is a certain logic to this, it puts a lot of your eggs in one basket and makes your home a considerable part of your overall financial portfolio. As we all know from recent experience, there is no guarantee housing prices will always go up. We believe it still makes sense to own your primary home, but making it too big a part of your overall financial picture means you may not have sufficient funds left over to do other kinds of investing.

Another risk of the buy-the-biggest-home-you-can philosophy is that it leaves you no buffer if things don't go exactly as planned. It assumes your salaries will always go up, but what if one of you is let go from work, or stops working to raise a child, or has to take an extended leave of absence for health reasons? You don't want to struggle to make your monthly payments because you bought more house than you could comfortably afford. So our suggestion is, buy a home but buy an affordable one that is within your means today and not some distant time in the future.

Of course reality don't always match up with what we might all agree on paper is the ideal. Our own first home purchase is a good example. At the time we were earning less than $40,000 *combined*. Our initial mortgage payment was $936 per month, which was right at the outer limit of the 28/36 rule ($40,000 x 28% = $11,200 ÷ 12 = $933). So we stretched financially just as far as we could in buying our own home.

But we essentially did things backwards – buying our home first, then investing in ourselves so our jobs improved and the monthly mortgage payments became less onerous. It would have been preferable to have the better jobs first, since more robust salaries make everything about owning a home and investing for retirement easier.

A Fine Time to Buy a Home

Mortgage interest rates are currently at historically low valuations: below 3% APR for a 15-year fixed-rate mortgage, and below 3.5% APR for a 30-year fixed-rate mortgage as of the first quarter of 2013.

Home prices, meanwhile, remain quite affordable. While they have recovered somewhat since the real estate bubble burst in 2007, valuations are still attractive compared to what they were before. The combination of reasonable home prices and historically low mortgage interest rates makes it a great time to consider buying a home.

We're not suggesting you speculate on homes per se, but if you're in the market for your primary home anyway and happen to find the one of your dreams, you should be able to buy it more affordably than you could have prior to 2007.

Saving Up for a Downpayment

So many financial obligations seem to hit all at once when you're young and just starting out. You want to buy your first home, educate yourself for a better future, pay off your debts, and start investing early, but it's hard to do all of that at the same time. How do you decide what comes first?

In terms of prioritizing we would advise you to: 1) invest in yourselves first so you can get decent-paying jobs right from the start, 2) pay off your debts, 3) save for a downpayment on an affordable home, and 4) start living in your home at the same time you start investing in earnest for retirement.

20% vs. 10% Downpayments

How much should you save up for a downpayment? The ideal is 20% – that's what lenders would prefer to see. But 20% of a $250,000 home is $50,000, and that's a fair chunk of change. If you can afford a 20% downpayment, then you get the best mortgage terms with the lowest interest rate, so that's the percentage we would recommend.

If that's not feasible, see if you can arrange a 10% downpayment with your bank. That amount is less daunting and will get you into your home in a shorter period of time. A 10% downpayment may be enough to qualify you for a loan, assuming you're debt-free otherwise and have solid credit scores. Keep in mind that if you start with a 10% downpayment and a high interest rate, you can always refinance to a lower-rate mortgage once your equity reaches 20%.

Private Mortgage Insurance

With downpayments of less than 20%, you're required to pay for mandatory supplemental insurance known as private mortgage insurance. PMI protects your lender against non-payment should you default on your loan. It typically amounts to 0.5% of the loan amount, so for a $250,000 mortgage that would amount to slightly over $100 extra per month. While it's no fun having to pay PMI, it's a relatively small price to pay for getting into your home sooner. PMI is payable until you reach 20% equity in your mortgage, then you can notify your lender to cancel it.

Leveraging Your Initial Investment

The huge benefit of home ownership is that you build equity in your home while getting to live in it. If you're lucky, you'll see the market value of your home increase over time, which means your equity will also increase.

Take our own situation. We bought our home in 1991 for just over $100,000 and sold it in 2007 for just under $300,000. Not only did we get to live in the home for

16 years, but at the end of that period we owned the home outright because we had refinanced from a 30-year to a 15-year mortgage and then completely paid the mortgage off. We were able to leverage a small initial investment (i.e., our downpayment) into a significant gain.

Small Downpayment, Big Rewards

A leveraged investment is any investment made with the use of borrowed money, allowing you to increase the potential return of the investment. By far the most common form of leveraging is the use of a mortgage to purchase a home.

Let's say you have a $100,000 condo and your downpayment is 20%. That's 5:1 leverage (since $20,000 is one fifth of $100,000). If your condo appreciates 5% over the course of the year, then you've just earned $5,000 on your initial $20,000 investment – a 25% return.

By comparison, let's say your downpayment is 10% instead of 20%. That's 10:1 leverage (since $10,000 is one-tenth of $100,000). If your condo appreciates the exact same 5%, you've just earned $5,000 on an initial $10,000 investment – a 50% return.

That's leveraging at work. Just like using a physical lever, you've managed to lift up something heavy with less effort. You benefit from the appreciation on the full value of the condo even though most of the money used to buy it was not yours but the lender's.

Why Leveraging Your Home Makes Sense

We believe primary home ownership is the one form of leveraged investment that really makes sense for the average investor. Leveraging magnifies both gains *and* losses, so you need to be careful using it if you don't want to get burned – for example, by buying on margin in the stock market.

However, when we're talking about your primary home, your risks are lower because you're living in the home presumably for the long term and have a high stake in making certain the monthly payments are made. Your risks are lower, too, if you buy a home within your financial comfort zone to begin with.

Owning vs. Renting

Our home turned out to be one of our best investments, so perhaps we're a bit biased, but we think home ownership makes great sense for the majority of people saving for early retirement. Your monthly mortgage payment remains fixed, which gives you something you can rely on during your investing years, and your home actually becomes part of your overall investment plan.

Home ownership is a forced savings plan of sorts that allows you to grow your wealth as the price of the property appreciates. In the end you can sell the home, downsize to something smaller, and use the remaining equity to help fund your retirement.

The one caution we have is this: if you think you may move locations over the short term – for job reasons, say – you might end up having to sell your home in a down market. For this reason you may want to wait until you're reasonably secure in your job before buying your home.

The Pros of Renting

Renting gives you increased flexibility with no long-term commitments. You have little or no responsibility or expense for maintenance, home improvements, or yard work. Your overall costs could conceivably be lower than owning a home if you manage to rent cheaply enough. And on top of all that, you avoid the need for a downpayment and a mortgage altogether, thus allowing you to start investing sooner.

We certainly believe it is possible to rent rather than own and still retire early. If you keep rental costs reasonably low and invest even more money than you would have otherwise in the markets to make up for the equity you won't have from owning a home, you can keep your life ultra-simple and still retire early. Depending on your lifestyle and where you live, renting could be the right answer for you.

The Cons of Renting

Perhaps the most significant downside of renting is that you can't control the rental price, which tends to go up with time. Your landlord determines what to charge, and sometimes the yearly increases can be dramatic. The same one-bedroom apartment we rented for $500 per month in 1991 now rents for $1,200 per month — more than double. Apartments in places like New York City and San Francisco have probably seen growth factors much higher than double over that same span of years.

By comparison, the costs of home ownership remain essentially steady with a fixed-rate mortgage. They may go up slightly due to small increases in insurance and property taxes, but the underlying mortgage rate itself remains fixed throughout. This stability is a comfort – something you can count on during your investing years.

Another downside of renting is that in the end you have nothing tangible to show for all the rental payments you've made over the years. It's as if all that money simply evaporated into thin air. Compare this to home ownership, where you build equity as you go and can take that equity with you once you sell your home. When we sold our home in 2007, we were able to put $200,000 into a bond fund and use the other $100,000 to buy a small condo. Downsizing allowed us to increase our liquid investments, which was just what we needed as early retirees relying on an income stream from those investments.

A third downside of renting is that you can't modify a rental property as you can a home. With rentals, what you see is typically what you get, from paint colors to appliances to flooring. But with homes you can make changes both to the home itself and to the land it sits on, which in turn can increase the home's final value.

Deducting Mortgage Interest

A final downside of renting is really more of an upside to owning: with a home you get to deduct mortgage interest payments from your itemized taxes, which you can't do with a rental. It's no wonder this has become the favorite tax deduction for millions of U.S. homeowners. A homeowner who spends $12,000 in interest payments and $3,000 in property taxes can deduct all $15,000 from his income taxes for the year.

The mortgage deduction benefit is most noticeable during the early years of your loan when you're paying the most in interest. Since interest lowers each year on an amortization schedule, one day you will reach a crossover point where the standard deduction ($12,200 in 2013 for a married couple filing jointly) is worth more than the mortgage interest deduction.

15-Year vs. 30-Year Mortgages

We recommend 15-year mortgages as a particularly good fit for those who hope to retire early. You'll save a lot on interest, and the 15 years matches up nicely with an early retirement goal. We think it's important to have your home completely paid off before you retire, and a 15-year mortgage lets you accomplish that.

Let's take a look at two different scenarios, one involving a 15-year and the other a 30-year fixed-rate mortgage, to get a sense of the difference in cost between the two. We'll assume a 20% downpayment on a $250,000 home, leaving a loan amount of $200,000. (By the way, we used mortgagecalculator.org to calculate the following two scenarios. You may want to use a calculator like this to run your own scenarios.)

Comparison of 30-year and 15-year Mortgages
($200,000 loan, 5% fixed interest rate)

Description	30-yr Fixed	15-yr Fixed
Monthly Payment	$1,334	$1,842
Total Number of Payments	360	180
Payoff Date (start date 2014)	2043	2028
Total Interest Paid	$186,512	$84,686
Total Property Tax Paid (1.25%)	$93,750	$46,875
Total Amount Paid	**$480,262**	**$331,561**

Note that we have assumed a 5% fixed interest rate for both loans. However, interest rates are typically *lower* for a 15-year mortgage than they are for a 30-year mortgage because of the shorter loan duration. The differences between the two examples would be even more dramatic if we had taken that into account, but it also would have made it harder to compare apples to apples.

Comparing Monthly Payment Amounts

Let's look first at the monthly payment amount. For a 30-year mortgage your monthly payment would be about $1,300, and for the 15-year mortgage it would be about $1,800. For a difference of about $500 per month you can cut 15 years off your mortgage.

Here's a fair question: What if the difference between the two payments is enough to put you outside the ideal range of the 20/28 rule we recommended earlier? We'll give you a partial answer here, but be sure to also read the following section on "unofficial" 15-year mortgages for what might be a better alternative.

We believe the benefits of doing a 15-year mortgage are so great compared to a 30-year mortgage that we would make an exception and recommend you stretch for the 15-year mortgage as long as your monthly payments remained within the 28% maximum required by the traditional 28/36 rule. That still puts you within the bounds of what mortgage lenders accept as the qualifying range for a loan, and in the end it will get you to your retirement goal faster.

Comparing Total Interest Paid

As noted above, interest rates are typically lower for a 15-year mortgage than they are for a 30-year mortgage. However, even when you assume the same 5% rate of interest for both mortgages, note the huge difference in the amount of total interest paid: approximately $187,000 versus $85,000. That's a difference of over $100,000 you don't have to pay if you go with a 15-year mortgage.

For the first several years of a 30-year mortgage, almost all you're paying is interest; you're hardly making a dent in the principal. But with a 15-year mortgage you make a noticeable dent in the principal right from the beginning. That means your equity grows faster, and your home is more your own and less the bank's.

If you should need to sell your home earlier than expected, your equity stake will be greater with the 15-year mortgage. You can use that higher stake to put a greater downpayment on your next home, keeping your borrowing costs lower.

Comparing Total Property Tax Paid

The total property tax paid for a 15-year mortgage is half what it is for a 30-year mortgage, but this is a bit misleading. You would have to continue paying property taxes on your home even after you paid off the 15-year mortgage, assuming you continued to live in it afterwards.

Under either scenario, if you ended up staying in the home for 30 years, the total property tax paid would be the same. However, if you sold the home after 15 years and downsized to a smaller property, your property taxes from that point forward would be comparably less. We pay a lot less in property taxes on our 400-square-foot condo than we did on our 1,800 square-foot home.

Comparing PMI Paid

The above comparison does not include private mortgage insurance, but if it did (i.e., because your downpayment was less than 20%, in which case PMI is required), then the total PMI paid for a 15-year loan would generally be less than half what it is for a 30-year loan. The reason is that you reach 20% equity in your mortgage much faster with the higher monthly principal payments you're making on a 15-year loan, and thus you can cancel the PMI sooner.

Comparing Total Amount Paid

When all is said and done, the total amount paid in the above comparison is about $480,000 for a 30-year mortgage versus $332,000 for a 15-year mortgage. That's a difference of nearly $150,000. We think it's worth an extra $500 per month in mortgage payments to save nearly $150,000, don't you?

Matching Your Mortgage to Your Retirement Date

If you know the exact retirement date you're shooting for, you can match the length of your home mortgage to that date. For example, if you plan to retire in 20 years, you could consider doing a 20-year mortgage.

That said, an equally attractive alternative is to stick with the 15-year mortgage even if you know you're going to retire in 20 years. That way the last five years before your retirement are completely mortgage-free, allowing you to save up even more money during those years – or spend a little more freely on travel and fun as you ease towards retirement.

Refinancing to a 15-Year Mortgage

If a 15-year mortgage is not financially feasible for you at first, you can always refinance to one after you've lived in your home for a period of time. However, be aware refinancing can involve steep finance charges. It's not unusual to pay 3% or more of your outstanding principal in refinancing fees. Thus refinancing often doesn't make sense unless you're paying a much higher interest rate than you would otherwise have to pay.

Refinancing made sense for us because we were paying an exceptionally high interest rate on our first loan, a 30-year FHA mortgage with 10% down. We refinanced to a 15-year mortgage once our equity reached the 20% mark. At that point we could qualify for a conventional loan with better interest rates. We were able to drop the PMI since we now had 20% equity, and we were able to get an extra-low interest rate because we were switching to a shorter-duration mortgage.

In the end we saved nearly $125,000 in interest charges by refinancing to a 15-year mortgage, and our monthly payments were only slightly higher than they were before. It would have been cleaner and cheaper to have started with a conventional mortgage in the first place, but sometimes you do what you have to do to make a beginning.

"Unofficial" 15-Year Mortgages

If the interest rate on your 30-year mortgage is already acceptably low, you can avoid refinancing charges by sticking with your 30-year mortgage but unofficially turning it into a 15-year mortgage by paying down the principal faster.

Making Extra Principal Payments

If you make extra payments towards the principal each month (or on a biweekly basis), that will have the effect of lowering your overall interest payments and reducing the term of the loan.

For instance, if you pay an extra $100 per month towards the principal on a $180,000 loan at 5% interest, your 30-year fixed-rate mortgage becomes in effect a 25-year mortgage. An extra $200 per month makes it the equivalent of a 20-year mortgage. An extra $450 per month gets you the equivalent of a 15-year mortgage without ever having to do the official paperwork to make it one.

An added benefit of this approach is that you're not locked into the extra payments. If you should find yourself temporarily unemployed, you could back off on making the extra payments for a period of time until you were re-employed. You thus have less risk of defaulting on your loan.

The only downside of this approach is human nature. It requires a good deal of self-discipline to keep making the voluntary payments through thick and thin, year after year. That said, if you are sufficiently motivated to retire early and have the discipline it takes, this can be a great solution.

In our own case, we switched to an "official" 15-year mortgage because of the better interest rates we could obtain, but we also made extra payments towards the principal of $100 per month, turning our 15-year mortgage into something closer to a 13-year mortgage. This let us retire a few years earlier than we could have otherwise because our mortgage was paid off sooner.

Prepayment Calculators

Mortgage amortization calculators like the one at HSH.com let you run different principal prepayment scenarios. Just plug different amounts into the "Monthly Additional Principal Prepayment Amount" box and hit "Calculate." You can quickly see the results of making different prepayments, including the total interest you will pay and the payoff date. This allows you to tailor your prepayment strategy to match your needs.

Staying Put in Your Home

Many people trade up from their first home, using it as a stepping stone to a bigger home, then trading up yet again to an even bigger one. Why, exactly? When you think of the energy and expense involved in packing and unpacking, remodeling and refurnishing, repainting and redecorating, and buying then buying again to suit the needs and dimensions of each bigger home, it makes you wonder what it's all for.

We suggest instead you stay put in your first home. Keep your life simpler and your needs smaller by staying in one place. Increase your existing home's value by making improvements to it inside and out. If you have no other choice but to move because of your job or some other necessity, then try moving sideways and buying a home that's comparable to the one you already have instead of upsizing.

Trading up for more and more home is counterproductive if you're seeking early retirement. Your goal is to *minimize* your expenses while maximizing your savings. Keeping your housing expenses as low as reasonably possible will let you achieve that goal with much less difficulty.

If you have kids or plan on having them, try to buy a first home big enough to accommodate them right from the beginning so you don't have to move to a bigger home later on. Of course no one has a crystal ball and all you can do is your best. Sometimes parents have no other choice but to buy a bigger home if they end up having more kids than expected.

If you buy a home that ends up being too big for your needs, you can always consider creative ways to use that extra space to your own advantage. For example, when we bought our home, we bought it with the intention of having children. We purchased an 1,800 square foot bi-level home with three bedrooms and two baths and a school just down the street. But when it turned out we couldn't have kids, we found ourselves with a lot more home than we needed. The bottom floor of the home was just sitting empty, so we decided to put it to good use and rent it out. In the end that extra space turned out to be a financial help to us as we saved for early retirement.

Is a Renter Right for You?

We were able to rent out the bottom half of our home for $550 per month. That extra $550 each month helped offset our mortgage costs during a time when money was tight and every dollar counted. In fact, it cut our monthly mortgage payments roughly in half, even after factoring in the taxes owed on the rental income.

If you're willing to entertain the possibility of having a renter, then consider first how your home is configured. Does it allow for a fair amount of privacy for you and your renter? Does it offer a separate entrance? Are there separate bathrooms with showers? Can you set up a mini-kitchen in the part of the home you'll be renting out? The more you can minimize the need to share space with your renter, the easier it will be for all parties.

Our bi-level home offered a good deal of privacy both for us and our renter, so the inconvenience was minor compared to the financial benefits of receiving a monthly rental check. Of course we were diligent about qualifying our renter before accepting him into our home (he was an older retired gentleman), and over the years he ended up becoming not just a renter but a friend. We even benefited from the relationship unexpectedly when he offered to watch our dog for us when we went away on trips.

We know many people feel strongly about not wanting to share their home with anyone else, and we recognize this may or may not be a right option for you. If you're uncomfortable with the thought of having a renter, perhaps you can give some thought to other ways you could use any extra space in your home that's just sitting empty. Maybe you can set up a small home business of some sort, for example. Let your creative juices flow when considering different ways of bringing in a little additional income on top of your regular salaries. Even a little extra income can go a long way when you're striving mightily to live below your means.

Downsizing When You Retire

You may want to consider selling your bigger home and downsizing to a smaller home or condo once you retire. As we touched on earlier, this allows you to take a portion of the equity built up in your home and invest it in a more liquid asset such as a bond fund.

Liquid assets are more usable assets for early retirees. You can take $10,000 out of a bond fund and use it for living expenses once you retire, but you can't take $10,000 out of your home in the same easy manner. You'd either have to take out a home equity loan (which means going back into debt) or rent out all or a part of your home (which can be inconvenient) to gain access to the same $10,000. But if you downsize after you retire, you can take whatever remains and invest it in a mutual fund offering both liquidity and an income stream.

One of the great benefits of home ownership under current law is that when it comes time to sell your primary home, you owe no taxes whatsoever on the first $250,000 of capital gains (or $500,000 for couples). This can be a godsend if you're looking for some extra money with which to cushion your nest egg once you retire.

Of course another option is to buy a smaller home or condo right from the start and stay in it even after you retire. If you decide to move to a different location, you could always trade sideways, buying another home or condo for about the same price. The benefits of this approach are, it keeps your home mortgage to a minimum (i.e., you never bought more home than you needed), your property taxes are lower, and your utility costs are lower since your square footage is less.

If you go the condo route, be sure to take into consideration monthly HOA fees. You'll want to make sure they're as low as reasonably possible since they are the equivalent of paying rent each month. A terrific deal on a condo can seem less terrific once you factor in these fees.

Keeping Car Expenses Low

Until we retired in 2006, we drove the same two cars for the entire period of time during which we saved for early retirement. To us it just didn't make sense to pour a lot of money into cars when we knew their value would only go down instead of up as they got older. We saw them as a way to get around and not much more. That kind of thinking helped us get to our goal more quickly than we would have otherwise.

The Real Cost of a New Car

The average price for a new car these days is over $30,000. If instead of a new car for $30,000, you were to buy a used one for $10,000, the remaining $20,000 could fund a whole year's worth of investing for retirement. If you're a couple and each of you decides to buy a used car for $10,000 instead of a new one for $30,000, that's $40,000 extra that could be put towards retirement savings.

Now let's suppose you have a 20-year retirement plan and your goal is to put away $20,000 per year on average. That's $400,000 total you need to invest, with the rest of your portfolio's growth coming from compounding. The $40,000 you could have saved by buying two used cars instead of two new ones represents *one-tenth* of your total investment amount.

That's the real cost of a new car. You could be trading in the chance to retire several years earlier.

Self-Financing

If you're buying a used car for $10,000 instead of a new one for $30,000, the possibility of self-financing becomes much more feasible. You could start a car fund and save up the whole amount ahead of time, paying for the car in cash and thereby avoiding the need to pay interest on a car loan.

Even if you only manage to save up half the amount, a loan of $5,000 is less intimidating to pay back (and pay back quickly) than a loan of $10,000 or more. The less debt you have hanging over you the better.

Sharing One Car or Going Carless

For most of our working years we each had a car since our jobs took us in different directions and we often worked different hours. But once we retired, we sold the two cars and bought a single used one for $11,000 that we now share. We find one car is sufficient for our needs now. Having just one means maintenance and repair expenses, licensing and registration fees, and auto insurance fees are all less than they would be otherwise.

For many people a car is a necessity during their working years, but if you can get by without one and rely on public transport instead, so much the better. When I worked in Denver for a number of years, I took an express bus into the city each day not only to lower my expenses but also to avoid the headaches of city driving.

Anyone living in a major city with a subway system should consider doing without a car simply to avoid the high expense of parking. If you only venture out of the city on rare occasions, consider renting a car just when you need one. It would almost certainly be cheaper than owning.

If you're a couple and one of you is lucky enough to be within biking distance of work, then you may be able to get by with one car instead of two. Not only will your costs go down, but you'll get some good exercise each day.

Buying a Used Car

Buying a used car is not particularly risky if you do your homework first. Armed with knowledge you can become an informed buyer. We suggest you start with Kelly Blue Book (kbb.com) or Edmunds (edmunds.com), which can supply you with the estimated price range for the car you're interested in buying.

Carfax (carfax.com) lets you check on a used car's vehicle history. Simply enter the VIN or the state and license plate number to pull up the record. The current cost is $35 for one car, $45 for up to five, and $50 for unlimited reports within 30 days.

A vehicle inspection from a local mechanic is frequently offered at a low cost as an incentive for future business. It's smart to have a mechanic look at a used car first before you buy it.

Using Craigslist to Buy or Sell a Car

Consider buying or selling your car on Craigslist (craigslist.com). The website's free classifieds offer a heavily used forum for buying and selling used cars and just about everything else under the sun. We sold our two cars in less than a week after posting ads on the site and were able to get the price we wanted. We also found our current used car via a posting on Craigslist. If you're a single woman, we would recommend bringing someone with you when buying or selling for safety reasons.

Be sure to post quality photos with your ad – it makes a big difference in terms of your success rate. You can repost your ad every 48 hours to move it to the top of the queue, which is worth doing since it increases your visibility to prospective buyers.

As a side note, we also sold most of our furniture and belongings through Craigslist when we sold our home. Posting a phone number in your ad works best; if you post an email address you get a fair amount of spam mixed in, but all the phone calls we received were genuine and from local residents.

Buying vs. Leasing

We do not recommend leasing a car instead of buying one. The long-term cost of leasing is virtually always more than the cost of buying. It stands to reason when you think about it. If you purchase a single car and drive it for a decade or more, you're going to do better cost-wise than if you lease several cars over that same period of time.

Most people we know who lease their cars turn them in every two or three years so they're always driving what amounts to a new or close-to-new car. But there's a price to be paid for that privilege. You rarely get something for nothing in this world.

What confuses many people, and understandably so, is that monthly lease payments are typically 30% to 60% *less* than regular car loan payments. This seems like a great deal at first glance, but it's deceptive because monthly lease payments *never end* as long as you are leasing the car.

Once you pay off a regular car loan, you own the car outright. Other than maintenance and repair costs, you can drive the car payment-free for years to come for as long as it remains road-worthy. Your loan costs are effectively spread out over the entire ownership period of the vehicle. Thus, even though a regular loan payment may seem higher when compared to a monthly lease payment, it's actually much lower when you take this into account.

Paying for Car Repairs

Consider repair costs carefully before deciding to trade in your older car for a newer one. It's true that repair costs are higher for older cars, but every extra year you can squeeze out of your existing car is one more year without monthly loan payments or a big capital expenditure to buy a newer one.

Paying a high car repair bill can be painful because it hits all at once and often out of the blue, but it is less painful if you mentally spread the cost out over all the extra months you'll get to drive the car once it's fixed.

Of course, at some point the transmission may blow or some other repair cost may be so high that it no longer makes sense to pour more money into a car that has little or no value left to it. At that point it's sensible to put it out to pasture and look for a replacement. Kelly Blue Book (kbb.com) can help you determine your car's current value and whether or not you should spring for expensive repairs.

Chapter 15.
Keep Your Life Portfolio Balanced

Like your investment portfolio, your life portfolio should be balanced. Whether your mix of living for today and living for tomorrow is balanced 50/50, or 60/40, or 70/30 is up to you, but a highly unbalanced portfolio is a risky portfolio. If you only live for today you'll be broke tomorrow, and if you only live for tomorrow you'll be miserable today. As with most things in life, the middle way is the best way.

Since most of us can't sprint all the way to early retirement, we have to pace ourselves for the long run. We have to take deep breaths along the way (vacations) and remember to hydrate (have fun). If we try to run too fast we risk exhausting ourselves and giving up. Slow and steady wins the race – and lets us enjoy the scenery along the way.

Splurge on What You Enjoy Most

Our advice is, figure out what you care about most in life and spend more freely in that area. For us that means spending more on travel and less on material possessions (other than camping equipment). If you feel you're depriving yourself of something you really love, you'll never be able to stick to your plan over the long run.

Whatever your passion is, you shouldn't have to give it up in order to retire early. We choose to spend our extra money on travel, but perhaps that's not your passion. If you feel about theater, or food and wine, or fixing up antique automobiles the way we do about travel, then perhaps that is your "splurge area" in life. Be sure to make a little extra room in your budget for it.

You *should* spend money on the things that matter most to you, but you should also spend less in the areas that don't. If you're living a balanced life, then you should be able to have fun today *and* save for tomorrow. It's not an either/or proposition.

Live a Little!

If you don't already have a bucket list of things you'd like to see and do before you die, we suggest you start one. Pull out a map and begin thinking about where you'd like to go. Add to it creative pursuits you'd like to try, experiences you'd like to have, and things you'd like to accomplish. Then get started checking off a few of those boxes while you're still fully employed. We suggest you give special priority to activities that are close to home (since you can do them more easily while still at work) and adventures that are physically demanding. Some of the most amazing experiences in life — bungee jumping, mountain treks, walking safaris, whitewater rafting, skydiving, and so forth — are most easily accomplished while you're still young and fit (not to mention fearless).

Of course, the more fun you have along the way, the more fit you will remain and the younger at heart you will be. We still hope to be having adventures even in our golden years, albeit of a more subdued nature. Think river cruising in Europe, extended RV trips in North America, island living in the South Pacific, and housesitting in a few of our favorite foreign countries like Italy and New Zealand.

Now here's a question: If you were to wait until you were 65 – "normal" retirement age – to get started on your bucket list, how much of it do you realistically think you'd get done? Probably not as much as you'd like, and maybe only a fraction of what you have listed. But if you get started now, you can make real inroads while you're still at work, then keep right on accelerating into early retirement and have a decent chance of doing rather than just dreaming about all the wonderful things on your list.

Enjoying life to the fullest is not contradictory with saving for the future. It's possible to do both if you balance work with play and mix in plenty of fun along the way. It's not necessary to sacrifice fun on the altar of the future: it's simply necessary to balance *fun* with *funding*.

Have Faith in Your Own Future

It's undeniable saving for the future takes faith. You have to have faith you'll still be alive and "still you" 15 to 20 years from now. That life will still be worth living and you'll still have your health. That your retirement plan will actually work as planned. That saving small amounts of money each month really can add up to big rewards later on. And that the markets will perform as expected over the long term to get you to your goal.

That's a lot of faith! It's safe to say you *have* to be an optimist to plan a decade or two in advance for early retirement.

Nevertheless, one of the reasons we like talking about retirement in 15 to 20 years is that, yes, it's a long way off, but at least it's imaginable and worth thinking about. Talking about something 15 years down the road isn't quite so elusive as talking about something 40 years down the road. ("Are you kidding me? I could be *dead* in 40 years!") At least a 30-year-old can measure 15 years as being two halves of his own life thus far and picture himself as not being too radically different by the time he reaches 45. But ask the average 20-something to picture himself at age 65 and he'll simply shake his head. It doesn't bear thinking about.

We encourage you to have at least a mustard seed of faith in your own future. Retiring early is not an impossible dream by any means. It is achievable by normal everyday people, as we ourselves can attest. If anyone tries to tell you you're missing out on life and wasting your time saving up for early retirement, tell them to think again. They're missing out on life if they *don't* save up to make their dreams come true.

Chapter 16.
Health Care in Retirement

What should I do about health care? This is the question every American who has ever thought about retiring early wants an answer to, and up until now it has been one of the hardest answers to provide. We say up until now because things are changing fast. New rules are coming into effect that are much more favorable to early retirees. In fact the new regulations open doors to health care that are closed to those currently covered by employee health plans.

By January 1, 2014, most provisions of the Patient Protection and Affordable Care Act will be in full effect, and at that point the health care outlook for early retirees on a budget will have improved dramatically. Affordable health care will no longer be tied inextricably to holding down a full-time job with benefits. What that means for those still working is more flexibility in deciding when to retire. For those already retired, it means a much better deal when it comes to paying premiums and receiving affordable health care benefits in return.

Over the past six years of early retirement, we estimate we've paid $23,000 in health care premiums while receiving no meaningful health care benefits in return. Our existing catastrophic policy's high deductible limits mean that in effect we've had to pay the full cost of every office visit to every doctor, dentist, or optometrist, every test or screening received, every filling filled and tooth crowned, and every prescription drug purchased. Our insurance provides us with financial protection more than true health care, but since one serious illness could wipe out our entire savings, we've felt we had little choice but to cover ourselves with some kind of policy, no matter how rudimentary.

Needless to say, we've tried to keep our health care visits to a minimum. It's virtually impossible to walk into a doctor's or dentist's office without walking out with a bill for $300 or more. We estimate we've spent $6,000 over the past six years on medical and dental services, and of course that number could have been dramatically higher if we hadn't been in reasonably good health.

But starting next year, for the first time in six years, we expect to receive actual benefits in return for the health care premiums we pay. Perhaps equally importantly, we can count on our premiums staying relatively stable over the years to come. Our premiums won't be much lower than they are now, but our deductibles will be significantly lower, and we'll only have to pay a co-pay instead of the entire bill if we make a visit to the doctor. We'll also have to pay less out of pocket if we should ever face a serious illness. In short, our health care coverage will feel a lot more like it did back in the days when we were covered under our old employee health care plans at work. That's no coincidence, since the new legislation is essentially designed to mimic the levels of coverage provided under most employee health care plans.

Key Aspects of the Affordable Care Act

Without question the Affordable Care Act is a game changer for early retirees on a budget. Practically speaking, it means one of the main roadblocks to early retirement – the lack of affordable health care – has finally been cleared away. Here's a summary of some of the key benefits of the act:

- **Guaranteed issue:** you cannot be denied coverage because of a preexisting condition or charged higher rates if you have a medical condition.
- **Subsidized premiums:** monthly premiums stay reasonable as you age (assuming annual income falls within certain limits, as discussed below).
- **Subsidized out-of-pocket expenses:** annual expenses for deductibles and coinsurance stay manageable (assuming income falls within certain limits).

- **Free preventive health services:** free services are offered for regular blood pressure and cholesterol checks, screenings for colon cancer and diabetes, well woman exams, and many other preventive tests.
- **Health care exchanges:** a single online marketplace for each state makes it easier to compare plan costs and benefits.

The act requires insurers to spend between 80% and 85% of every premium dollar on medical care (as opposed to administration, advertising, etc.). If insurers exceed this threshold, they have to rebate any excess to their customers. This aspect of the new law is already in effect, and the nation's health insurance companies have already refunded over $1 billion to their customers.

The information in this section is based primarily on data provided on the government's health care website, HealthCare.gov, and the Kaiser Family Foundation's *Summary of New Health Reform Law*. We've made every effort to be as accurate as possible in our description of how the new regulations affect early retirees, but any errors are wholly our own and we can only say we did our best to explain in a straightforward fashion a rather complicated piece of legislation.

Guaranteed Issue

Under the Affordable Care Act all discrimination against pre-existing conditions is prohibited. You cannot be denied affordable coverage due to your health, and your insurance will actually have to cover you should a medical need arise, without concern that some paperwork error might result in a cancellation of coverage. Most would agree this is a significant improvement over the previous state of affairs.

According to the Kaiser Family Foundation, over one-fifth of people who applied for health insurance on their own in the past got turned down, or were charged a higher price, or were offered a plan that excluded coverage for their pre-existing condition. But the days of cherry-picking only the healthiest customers are past. Insurance companies can no longer put annual limits on essential health benefits such as hospital stays, nor can they put a lifetime cap on the amount of care they are willing to cover.

Differences in premiums based on gender are also prohibited. Gender discrimination, something that was only proscribed by law in one-fifth of the states, is now banned in all fifty states. That means women will no longer have to pay premiums that were sometimes 50% to 100% higher than men's.

Free Preventive Care

All new plans must cover certain preventive services without charging a deductible, co-pay, or coinsurance. These services include screenings for blood pressure, cholesterol, diabetes, and HIV as well as routine vaccinations, flu and pneumonia shots, mammograms, pap smears, and colonoscopies. The official government website at HealthCare.gov provides a full list of preventive care services.

The act makes it possible for all Americans to avail themselves of proven preventive measures without having to think twice about whether they can afford it. Women in particular are beneficiaries of the new law, since private health plans must now provide free well-woman visits, new baby care, breastfeeding supplies, contraception, and many types of screenings at no charge. Some specifics are still being worked out, but the overall intent is clear: to make it easier for women to get the basic health care services they need irrespective of their financial situation.

Required Health Insurance

Virtually all citizens will be required to have basic health insurance beginning in 2014 or else pay a federal tax penalty. The provision is intended to drive down health care costs by spreading the expense of health care over a larger pool of people, including younger and healthier adults who might otherwise decline purchasing insurance. Of course, younger adults will turn older themselves someday and will likely require more medical care in the future, so while they might understandably grumble about the new law over the short term, they stand a reasonable chance of benefiting from it over the long term.

Those who refuse coverage will have to pay a tax penalty of $95 per individual, $285 per family, or 1% of income (whichever is greater) in 2014. Those penalty amounts increase to $695 per individual, $2,085 per family, or 2.5% of income (whichever is greater) by 2016. After 2016 the penalty increases annually based on cost-of-living adjustments. Exclusions apply for individuals who make too little money to file a federal tax return, or who would have to spend more than 8% of their household income on the cheapest qualifying plan.

Americans living abroad are exempt from having to purchase health insurance or pay any associated penalties. However, the definition of living abroad appears to be fairly strict. You must be a bona fide resident of a foreign country in order to opt out. The rules seem to suggest you must be "an individual whose tax home is in a foreign country," *and* you must reside in a foreign country or countries for at least 330 full days out of the year in order to be exempt. Clarifications may eventually point to a less restrictive interpretation, but for now it appears that simply traveling in foreign countries for extended periods of time (i.e., six months or more) is not enough in and of itself to exempt you from having to either pay for basic health insurance or else pay a penalty.

How Premiums and Out-of-Pocket Limits Are Determined

Now we get into the nitty-gritty of how your health care premiums and out-of-pocket maximums are determined under the new law. It's worth noting up front that you don't have to wait until you submit your taxes to claim your premium subsidies under the Affordable Care Act. Rather, subsidies are "advanceable," which means they are built right into the reduced premiums you pay on a monthly basis once you enroll in a qualified health care plan. The tax credit is sent directly to your insurance company and applied to your premium, so you immediately pay less out of pocket.

Subsidies and the Federal Poverty Level

To understand how the Affordable Care Act applies to you as an early retiree, you have to begin, strangely enough, with the federal poverty level. That's because subsidies for monthly health care premiums (and annual out-of-pocket limits) are tied to the federal poverty level.

Summarized in the shaded boxes below are the 2013 federal poverty guidelines for households of one to four people for the 48 contiguous states. Start with your household size, then note the annual income limits specified under the baseline 100% column.

Household Size	Percentage of Federal Poverty Guidelines (2013)					
	100%	133%	150%	200%	300%	400%
1	$11,490	$15,282	$17,235	$22,980	$34,470	$45,960
2	$15,510	$20,628	$23,265	$31,020	$46,530	$62,040
3	$19,530	$25,975	$29,295	$39,060	$58,590	$78,120
4	$23,550	$31,322	$35,325	$47,100	$70,650	$94,200

As the 100% column shows, the official poverty level for residents of the continental U.S. is $11,490 for a single individual and $15,510 for a couple (as of 2013). These amounts are typically adjusted each year by the Department of Health and Human Services to account for inflation.

Now read across the row that applies to the number of people in your household. As long as your income falls within 400% of the federal poverty level, your health care premiums are capped on a sliding scale that goes no higher than 9.5% of your annual household income. (Technically the sliding scale is based on "modified adjusted gross income," but this is the same as gross income for the majority of households). Annual out-of-pocket limits are also subsidized as long as your income falls below the 400% mark.

What this means for you as an early retiree is that you may want to manage your income level to keep it below 400% of the poverty line – in other words, $45,960 for one person or $62,040 for a couple as of 2013 – in order to be eligible for premium assistance. As soon as you cross the 400% threshold, the subsidy immediately drops to zero. Thus it is crucial to stay below this mark if at all possible if you want to qualify for a subsidized premium and lower your maximum out-of-pocket expenses as well.

Subsidized Health Care Premiums

Let's take a closer look at how health care premiums work under the Affordable Care Act. We'll start with an example. Let's say you are a married couple 50 years of age and your annual income is $62,000 per year. That means you're bumping right up against the 400% limit as shown in the previous table, so your annual health care premiums are capped at 9.5% of your income. That's $62,000 x 9.5% = $5,890 per year, or $491 per month.

But if you earn just $1,000 more and have an annual income of $63,000, the subsidy immediately drops to zero. Suddenly you need to pay the full cost of the monthly premium, and the premium without subsidies for a couple your age is likely to run about $15,420 per year, or $1,285 per month (based on national estimates by the Congressional Budget Office). That's a difference of nearly $10,000 per year or $800 per month. So you can see how important it is to keep your annual income within the 400% limit if you are anywhere close to that limit to begin with.

Here's the good news, though. If you are an early retiree living on a budget, then whether you are age 44 or 54 or 64, your premiums are *always* capped based on your income level as long as you stay within 400% of the poverty level. That means your premiums won't skyrocket as you get older. Instead your premium costs will stay roughly the same, other than rising with overall increases in health care costs and inflation. As you age, more and more of the premium amount will be subsidized. That means you will continue to receive affordable health care even between the ages of 55 and 64 when premiums tend to be at their highest. Once you hit age 65, of course, you qualify for Medicare.

Think about how important this is for early retirees on a budget: it means they no longer have to worry about skyrocketing premiums as they grow older. Speaking for ourselves, we were dreading the super-high premiums we knew were coming just around the bend. In fact we had been considering dropping U.S. health coverage altogether during those years and relying instead solely on medical care overseas. But as long as the Affordable Care Act remains law, the days of exorbitant premiums for most Americans age 55 to 64 are a thing of the past.

Age and the 3:1 Ratio

The Affordable Care Act stipulates that the most expensive policies for older individuals can be no more than three times the price of policies for younger adults. Thus a 64-year-old would have to pay no more than three times what a 20-year-old would pay for the same coverage.

The 3:1 rule is easiest to understand if you consider two individuals, aged 20 and 64, both with incomes higher than 400% of the poverty limit and therefore unable to qualify for premium subsidies. If the 20-year-old pays a premium of, say, $200 per month, then by law insurance companies cannot charge the 64-year-old more than $600 per month. The end result of the 3:1 rule is that younger participants will pay more for health insurance than they would have otherwise, while older participants will pay less. In essence, the burdens of higher health care costs that come with growing older have been spread out more evenly across the entire pool of insured.

Keep in mind the 3:1 ratio applies primarily to *unsubsidized* policies. Once you reach a cap for your income level, you can't go higher than that, period. For example, if a couple in their twenties and a couple in their sixties both have incomes of $60,000 (meaning they both fall just within the 400% limit), they would both pay the same premium amount of $475 per month ($60,000 x 9.5% income cap = $5,700 ÷ 12 = $475). The difference is that the couple in their twenties would receive premium subsidy assistance of about $40 per month, while the couple in their sixties would receive premium subsidy assistance of about $1,040 per month. While the level of assistance differs dramatically behind the scenes, the two couples pay the same monthly premiums up front.

The Sliding Scale

So far we've discussed how premiums work for people bumping right up against the 400% level of the poverty limit. But what if your income falls somewhere lower in the spectrum, say, at the 250% mark? The simple answer is that you would pay less based on a sliding scale. Premium caps begin at just 2% of income if your annual income is less than 133% of the poverty level, and they climb steadily from there up to the maximum 9.5% cap. The following table shows the premium cap percentages that apply as your annual income increases.

Percent of Poverty Limit	Premium Capped At x% of Income	Individual		Couple	
		Income Range	Max Annual Premium	Income Range	Max Annual Premium
100-133%	2.0%	$11,490 – $15,282	$230 – $306	$15,510 – $20,628	$310 – $413
133-150%	3.0% – 4.0%	$15,282 – $17,235	$458 – $689	$20,628 – $23,265	$619 – $931
150-200%	4.0% – 6.3%	$17,235 – $22,980	$689 – $1,448	$23,265 – $31,020	$931 – $1,954
200-250%	6.3% – 8.05%	$22,980 – $28,725	$1,448 – $2,312	$31,020 – $38,775	$1,954 – $3,121
250-300%	8.05% – 9.5%	$28,725 – $34,470	$2,312 – $3,275	$38,775 – $46,530	$3,121 – $4,420
300-400%	9.5%	$34,470 – $45,960	$3,275 – $4,366	$46,530 – $62,040	$4,420 – $5,894
>400%	No Cap	> $45,960	No Cap	> $62,040	No Cap

Based on 2013 federal poverty guidelines

The table illustrates, for example, that a married couple with income of $40,000 per year would fall between 250% and 300% of the poverty limit, and thus their premium would be capped on a sliding scale between 8.05% and 9.5% of their annual income. As shown in the right-hand column, their maximum annual premium would therefore fall between $3,121 and $4,420 per year, or between $260 and $368 per month.

To get an even more exact idea, you can multiply your specific annual income (e.g., $40,000) by 8.05% then by 9.5% to ascertain the range of your maximum annual premium (e.g., $3,220 to $3,800 per year, or $268 to $317 per month).

Out-of-Pocket Maximums

Unlike monthly health care premiums that must be paid regardless of how much or how little one uses the health care system, out-of-pocket expenses are tied to actual visits to doctors and hospitals and such. If you make no such visits and purchase no prescription drugs, then your annual out-of-pocket costs may well be zero or close to zero. But if you make frequent visits to the doctor or face a sudden medical emergency, your out-of-pocket expenses may be significantly higher.

Fortunately, these expenses are capped on an annual basis under the law. Maximums under the Affordable Care Act are based on out-of-pocket limits already established by the IRS each year for Health Savings Accounts (tax-advantaged accounts associated with high-deductible health care plans). Out-of-pocket HSA limits for 2013, for example, are $6,250 for an individual and $12,500 for a family.

These same limits have been adopted for health care plans under the Affordable Care Act. These are the *unsubsidized* maximums any person or family enrolled in a qualified health care plan should have to pay out of pocket in any given year, no matter what their income level. Once the maximum is reached, your plan pays for all covered expenses beyond that point.

Just like health care premiums, out-of-pocket limits are subsidized under the Affordable Care Act based on income level. Subsidies apply as long as your income falls within 400% of the federal poverty level. Beyond 400% the subsidy immediately drops to zero. As shown in the following table, your maximum out-of-pocket expenses may be one-third, one-half, or two-thirds of the current-year HSA limit, depending on where your household income falls in relation to the federal poverty level.

Percent of Poverty Limit	Annual Out-of-Pocket Maximums	Out-of-Pocket Maximum per Individual	Out-of-Pocket Maximum per Couple
100-200%	⅓ of HSA limit	$6,250 x ⅓ = $2,083	$12,500 x ⅓ = $4,167
200-300%	½ of HSA limit	$6,250 x ½ = $3,125	$12,500 x ½ = $6,250
300-400%	⅔ of HSA limit	$6,250 x ⅔ = $4,167	$12,500 x ⅔ = $8,333

Based on 2013 federal poverty guidelines

Health Care Calculators

The information in the previous section gives you a behind-the-scenes look at how your health care premiums and out-of-pocket maximums are determined, but it will all be much simpler once 2014 rolls around. Then, when you consider a particular insurance plan online, it will let you know your estimated premium and annual out-of-pocket maximum once you have plugged in basic information about yourself.

In fact, health care calculators are already available that will do most of the work for you. The one we like best is the National Health Care Calculator provided by UC Berkeley Labor Center (laborcenter.berkeley.edu/healthpolicy/calculator). You simply plug in your household size, annual income, and age and it instantly estimates your monthly premium. The example on the following page is based on our own inputted information.

```
┌─Calculator─────────────────────────────────────────────────────┐
│                                                                 │
│          Number of family members (1-8)          │2        │   │
│                                                                 │
│                 Annual family income             │40,000   │   │
│                                                                 │
│     Age of policyholder (ages 19-64 only)        │49       │   │
│                                                                 │
│                 Federal poverty level             258%          │
│                                                                 │
├─Monthly Premium─────────────────────────────────────────────────┤
│                                                                 │
│              Total Premium, No Subsidy            $1,436        │
│                                                                 │
│     Maximum % of Income Towards Premium                         │
│                                                   8.3%          │
│                 Premium Cost to Family                          │
│                                                   $276          │
│                Federal Premium Subsidy                          │
│                                                   $1,160        │
│                                                                 │
└─────────────────────────────────────────────────────────────────┘
```

The calculator shows that we fall at 258% of the poverty level and that our total estimated health care premium *without* subsidy would be $1,436 per month for a "Silver-level" plan (discussed in the next section). Since actual premiums aren't known yet, these are based on national estimates from the Congressional Budget Office. The calculator indicates that the most we should have to spend on health care premiums is 8.3% of our annual income, or $276 per month. (The manual calculation would be $40,000 x 8.3% = $3,320 ÷ 12 = $276.)

The difference between the premium without subsidy ($1,436) and the premium with subsidy ($276) is $1,160 per month. Thus the federal premium subsidy amounts to an estimated $13,920 per year.

Part of the utility of calculators like these is being able to plug in different values to see how they affect (or don't affect) your premium. For instance, changing the age in the example above from 49 to either 19 or 64 (the lowest and highest ages you can enter) has no effect whatsoever on the premium. Instead, what changes dramatically is the amount of the *subsidy*. It's also educational to plug in amounts slightly higher than the 400% limit and see how the monthly premium instantly shoots upwards once the subsidies disappear.

Bronze, Silver, Gold, and Platinum Plans

Beginning in 2014, health care plans will be offered at four different coverage levels: Bronze, Silver, Gold, and Platinum. Platinum plans have the highest premiums but the lowest out-of-pocket costs. Gold, Silver, and Bronze plans each in turn have lower monthly premiums but cost increasingly more out of pocket. The color coding helps you quickly identify the type of health care plan that best suits your needs.

The lowest-cost plan may not always be the best plan for you. For instance, Bronze-level plans have the lowest monthly premiums, but out-of-pocket expenses are *unsubsidized* no matter what your income level. Instead, out-of-pocket limits simply match whatever the current HSA limit is (e.g., $6,250 for individuals and $12,500 for families in 2013). So while Bronze-level plans may have the lowest premium cost, they may not always represent the best value.

In the end, of course, best value depends on the details of your own personal situation – your health, your income level, your likely frequency of medical care visits, and so forth. For people with ongoing medical conditions, the Gold or Platinum plans might represent best value even after factoring in the higher premium costs. Then, too, none of us knows when an unexpected medical emergency might occur, and that might be reason enough to consider going with a slightly more expensive plan.

The second-lowest-level Silver plans are especially worth considering if you are an early retiree on a budget. These plans are typically used as baseline models in illustrations about the Affordable Care Act because they represent a good balance between coverage and cost. For many people they may represent the best value.

Under Silver-level plans, both health care premiums *and* out-of-pocket maximums are subsidized (assuming your income falls within 400% of the federal poverty limit). Your level of cost sharing is also less with a Silver plan than it is with a Bronze plan, as discussed below.

Cost Sharing Under Different Color Tiers

Each color tier – Bronze, Silver, Gold, Platinum – has been designed with a different percentage of cost sharing in mind. Cost sharing has to do with how much you spend out of pocket versus how much your plan covers. Deductibles, coinsurance, co-pays, and any other point-of-service charges all go into the cost sharing equation. By design, each color tier has its own "actuarial value," which is an estimate of the overall financial protection provided by a health plan across a standard population of both healthy and sick consumers. Here are the actuarial values that each color tier is designed to meet:

- Bronze: 60%
- Silver: 70%
- Gold: 80%
- Platinum: 90%

Because we're talking averages here, the percentage listed for each color tier does not necessarily represent the exact amount your plan will pay *you* as an individual enrollee. Rather, it represents what percentage the plan is likely to pay on average across a large group of people, both healthy and sick.

In general, though, it's safe to say that the higher the percentage, the more your out-of-pocket medical expenses will be covered over the course of a year. Everything from deductibles to co-pays to coinsurance percentages will be less. On the other hand, you'll have to pay up front for those benefits with higher monthly premiums.

If your income falls within 400% of the federal poverty level, you may want to consider one of the higher-level plans (Silver, Gold, or Platinum) because they may represent a better value for you. The result of all those subsidies and cost-sharing reductions is that you gain access to a higher-quality plan than you might otherwise be able to afford.

As an extreme example, if your income falls within 150% of the poverty level, you can take advantage of a Platinum plan with an actuarial value of 94% once all cost sharing measures and subsidies have been factored in. What that means, essentially, is that you have to spend very little money to get quite a lot of coverage.

Note that plans within each color tier will not be exactly identical to each other because there is more than one way for a Silver plan, say, to reach an actuarial value of 70%. One plan may offer a higher deductible but with lower coinsurance, while another might have a lower deductible but higher coinsurance. Each achieves the same actuarial value in different ways. This is actually a good thing for consumers, because it gives them more choice in finding the plan that best fits their needs.

Health Insurance Exchanges

By January 1, 2014, each state is required to have a Health Insurance Exchange set up that will allow you to easily compare health care coverage from competing plans and select the one that best fits your needs. Each plan will provide a "Summary of Benefits and Coverage" that quickly allows you to see what each plan offers. On the following page is a generic example of the type of information that will be provided on the first few pages of these plans. (Source: www.dol.gov/ebsa/pdf/SBCSampleCompleted.pdf.)

With these overviews you can quickly assess your deductible and out-of-pocket limits and tell what a visit to the doctor will cost, what a diagnostic or imaging test will run, what generic drugs will cost as compared to brand-name drugs, and what your coinsurance will be for outpatient and hospital stays. The only thing not specifically listed is the monthly premium, and that will be provided at the Health Insurance Exchange's top level before you reach this more detailed information.

Important Questions	Answers	Why this Matters:
What is the overall deductible?	**$500** person / **$1,000** family. Doesn't apply to preventive care	You must pay all the costs up to the **deductible** amount before this plan begins to pay for covered services you use. Check your policy or plan document to see when the **deductible** starts over (usually, but not always, January 1st). See the chart starting on page 2 for how much you pay for covered services after you meet the **deductible**.
Are there other deductibles for specific services?	Yes. **$300** for prescription drug coverage. There are no other specific **deductibles**.	You must pay all of the costs for these services up to the specific **deductible** amount before this plan begins to pay for these services.
Is there an out-of-pocket limit on my expenses?	Yes. For participating providers **$2,500** person / **$5,000** family. For non-participating providers **$4,000** person / **$8,000** family	The **out-of-pocket limit** is the most you could pay during a coverage period (usually one year) for your share of the cost of covered services. This limit helps you plan for health care expenses.
What is not included in the out-of-pocket limit?	Premiums, balance-billed charges, and health care this plan doesn't cover.	Even though you pay these expenses, they don't count toward the **out-of-pocket limit**.
Is there an overall annual limit on what the plan pays?	No.	The chart starting on page 2 describes any limits on what the plan will pay for *specific* covered services, such as office visits.
Does this plan use a network of providers?	Yes. See www.[insert].com or call 1-800-[insert] for a list of participating providers.	If you use an in-network doctor or other health care **provider**, this plan will pay some or all of the costs of covered services. Be aware, your in-network doctor or hospital may use an out-of-network **provider** for some services. Plans use the term in-network, **preferred**, or participating for **providers** in their **network**. See the chart starting on page 2 for how this plan pays different kinds of **providers**.
Do I need a referral to see a specialist?	No. You don't need a referral to see a specialist.	You can see the **specialist** you choose without permission from this plan.

Common Medical Event	Services You May Need	Your Cost If You Use a Participating Provider	Your Cost If You Use a Non-Participating Provider	Limitations & Exceptions
If you visit a health care provider's office or clinic	Primary care visit to treat an injury or illness	$35 copay/visit	40% coinsurance	none
	Specialist visit	$50 copay/visit	40% coinsurance	none
	Other practitioner office visit	20% coinsurance for chiropractor and acupuncture	40% coinsurance for chiropractor and acupuncture	none
	Preventive care/screening/immunization	No charge	40% coinsurance	
If you have a test	Diagnostic test (x-ray, blood work)	$10 copay/test	40% coinsurance	none
	Imaging (CT/PET scans, MRIs)	$50 copay/test	40% coinsurance	none
If you need drugs to treat your illness or condition More information about **prescription drug coverage** is available at www.[insert].	Generic drugs	$10 copay/prescription (retail and mail order)	40% coinsurance	Covers up to a 30-day supply (retail prescription); 31-90 day supply (mail order prescription)
	Preferred brand drugs	20% coinsurance (retail and mail order)	40% coinsurance	none
	Non-preferred brand drugs	40% coinsurance (retail and mail order)	60% coinsurance	none
	Specialty drugs	50% coinsurance	70% coinsurance	none
If you have outpatient surgery	Facility fee (e.g., ambulatory surgery center)	20% coinsurance	40% coinsurance	none
	Physician/surgeon fees	20% coinsurance	40% coinsurance	none
If you need immediate medical attention	Emergency room services	20% coinsurance	20% coinsurance	none
	Emergency medical transportation	20% coinsurance	20% coinsurance	none
	Urgent care	20% coinsurance	40% coinsurance	none
If you have a hospital stay	Facility fee (e.g., hospital room)	20% coinsurance	40% coinsurance	none
	Physician/surgeon fee	20% coinsurance	40% coinsurance	none

Medical and Dental Tourism

The costs of health and dental care can be radically lower overseas – so much so that even after factoring in the expense of transportation there and back, it can still cost significantly less to have a procedure performed abroad than it would be to have the same procedure performed in the U.S.

Many who have received medical treatment abroad write glowing reports about their experiences and say they wished they had discovered such options sooner. What they find more often than not isn't some poor cousin of American health care, but rather top-notch medical facilities, superbly trained physicians with impeccable credentials, and staff who speak clear English and provide a level of personal service and care that would be hard to duplicate in the U.S. due to stark differences in costs.

If you like the idea of world travel as much as we do, then receiving at least some of your medical or dental care abroad is an appealing option. For example, we've taken advantage of dental care services and prescription drug bargains in Algodones, Mexico (just across the border from Yuma, Arizona) and have only good things to say about the experience. In this section we'll share some of our own experiences and point you towards some of the best countries in the world when it comes to medical tourism.

Medical Tourism and the Affordable Care Act

Even with the advent of the Affordable Care Act, we believe medical tourism will continue to thrive by offering deals that are simply too good to pass up. For example, certain elective surgeries at Thailand's Bumrungrad Hospital cost only one-tenth of what they do in the U.S., and a knee or hip replacement in India may still run you less than the amount of your annual out-of-pocket maximum in the U.S. As long as these kinds of dramatic cost differentials exist, medical tourism will continue to flourish.

The "Medical Tourism" website (medicaltourism.com) offers useful comparison costs for the same procedures in different countries. While costs are approximate, they are still quite an eye-opener, especially when you realize they already build in the estimated expense of airfare for two. Another useful website with dozens of helpful links about medical tourism is the Retire Early Lifestyle website run by early retirees Billy and Akaisha Kaderli (retireearlylifestyle.com/medical_tourism).

Admittedly, mandatory coverage under the Affordable Care Act does put something of a damper on medical tourism, since U.S. citizens are already invested to a certain extent in the health care system in this country. After all, not only are you paying a monthly premium, but you may also have a subsidized out-of-pocket limit that eliminates annual health care expenses beyond a certain point.

For example, even if a heart bypass surgery costs $15,000 in Thailand compared to $150,000 in the U.S. – a whole order of magnitude's difference – U.S. citizens might think twice before paying the $15,000 in Thailand since their subsidized annual out-of-pocket limit might only be $7,500, say, in the U.S. They know their insurance will cover the rest of the amount, so there is no incentive for them to seek treatment overseas since their personal costs would actually be higher.

Medical tourists from the U.S. may therefore end up migrating towards elective surgeries and specialized treatments that aren't covered by their insurance at home – things like cosmetic surgery, dental implants, Lasik surgery, in-depth wellness exams, groundbreaking stem cell therapies, and innovative cancer treatments that aren't yet covered by U.S. insurance.

Wherever gaps in coverage exist, or whenever procedures can be performed for less than out-of-pocket maximums, medical tourism will continue to offer a viable alternative. Any surgery that involves a long waiting period for whatever reason might also offer strong incentive for medical tourism to places like India, Thailand, or Malaysia where the surgery could be performed almost immediately.

Early retirees living beyond the 400% federal poverty limit remain particularly good candidates for continued medical care abroad. The Affordable Care Act doesn't help them as much as it does their less affluent brethren. They don't receive subsidies, for example, that reduce their annual out-of-pocket limits. That means their out-of-pocket costs could be as high as $6,250 for individuals or $12,500 for families, based on current-year limits.

If well-off retirees can receive a medical procedure overseas for substantially less than these limits, then they are likely to consider it. The only downside is that they're paying a monthly premium for services they aren't really utilizing, and the dollars that would have gone towards meeting their out-of-pocket limits for the year have gone somewhere else instead.

What About Simply Paying the Penalty Tax?

Some early retirees may be wondering whether it makes sense to simply pay the penalty tax and not have health care in America, relying instead solely on overseas care. While worth pondering, it's not a step to be taken lightly. Speaking for ourselves, we would be more than a little nervous about living in the U.S. for as many months as we do with no upper limit on our health care expenses. What if a sudden emergency should hit and we couldn't get overseas to address it? Then our health care costs could quickly skyrocket.

To our minds, the only way such a step might be worth considering is if we already spent the vast majority of our time overseas. Otherwise the approach seems too fraught with risks. A better option might be to purchase the cheapest Bronze-level plan available and balance that with overseas medical treatment when appropriate. Alternatively, you could consider taking the necessary steps to establish residency abroad in order to avoid the need for U.S. health care altogether.

Which Countries Are Best?

Some countries consistently make the top ten lists when it comes to medical and dental tourism. Here is a quick rundown of the best of the best based on our recent review of top ten lists posted by International Living, Forbes, Healthy Times Blog, Business Pundit, Medical Travel Quality Alliance, and more:

- **Thailand** is at or near the top of most lists. Bumrungrad Hospital just west of Bangkok has been called the crown jewel of medical tourism. Bangkok Hospital is another. You can recuperate after your procedure on one of Thailand's many lovely beaches.
- **Malaysia** is particularly famous for its "well man" and "well woman" preventive care packages that include extensive physicals and a battery of tests at a fraction of western costs. Malaysia also has its share of pristine beaches.
- **Singapore** is a third powerhouse in Southeast Asia, offering some of the best treatment centers in the world (e.g., Gleneagles Hospital) for serious issues ranging from cardiology to oncology to stem cell therapy.
- **India** is known for high-quality cardiac and orthopedic procedures at low cost. Medical and dental tourism are both growing rapidly here. Bangalore's Fortis Hospital is ranked as one of the best surgical centers in the world for medical travelers.
- **Mexico** is the ultimate close-to-home destination for Americans. Convenience and reasonable prices combine for a great solution when it comes to dental, vision, and prescription drug services, as well as routine physicals and tests and certain operations such as knee and hip replacements.
- **Costa Rica** is another popular destination for Americans, with a particular emphasis on dental care and cosmetic surgery. It offers "medical spas" in a safe, convenient, English-speaking, and ecologically beautiful country.
- **Hungary** is a prime European destination especially when it comes to dental tourism. Germans have been crossing the border for years for quality dental and medical care. Dental procedures can cost half what they do in most western countries.
- **Turkey** makes most top-ten lists because of its high number of accredited medical facilities, low cost, and western-trained doctors fluent in English. Turkey is especially known for eye treatments like Lasik surgery and for dental vacations.

The above eight countries make most top-ten lists on a consistent basis, but the last two countries tend to vary quite a bit. **South Korea** is on many lists as yet another Southeast Asian country offering state-of-the-art medical services, as well as the **Philippines**. **Panama** frequently makes the cut for destinations close to the U.S., and **Guatemala** is an up-and-comer. **Brazil** is well regarded for plastic surgery at a low price, as is **Egypt**. Another good option is **South Africa**, which offers tempting medical safaris. **Israel** makes some lists for its low-cost cancer treatment centers. Other popular European destinations for medical tourism include **Poland**, the **Czech Republic**, **Lithuania**, and **Spain**.

As you can see, the list of countries is extensive, and these are far from the only quality options when it comes to affordable medical and dental care abroad. Use this list as a starting point, but a quick web-based search will reveal many other fine options.

If you like the idea of medical tourism but don't actually want to go abroad, here's one final option: the Surgery Center of Oklahoma. This state-of-the-art multi-specialty facility offers up-front and bundled (all-inclusive) pricing posted online for all to see (surgerycenterok.com). It intentionally works outside the confines of the big hospital/insurance environment and strives for price transparency and affordability. Those with high deductibles or high out-of-pocket limits may find this a viable alternative and one more good option worth considering.

Dental Tourism

The extent of dental coverage under the Affordable Care Act is still something of a mystery. If it turns out such coverage is minimal or nonexistent under many plans, then affordable options abroad will offer an important alternative for early retirees.

Where dental tourism shines most brightly is when it comes to costly procedures such as root canals, crowns, implants, veneers, and bleaching. We can speak to this issue personally since Robin recently received a root canal, post and core, and porcelain-and-metal crown in Algodones, Mexico for a total price of $530. This compares quite well to the two quotes we received from dentists in the U.S. for $1,400 and $1,850 for the same work and materials.

Robin's experience was such a positive one that I plan to return to her dentist in the near future for an implant and crown. This procedure would generally cost $3,000 or more in the U.S., whereas we received a quote of $1,200 total from her dentist in Algodones (with some quotes being lower than $1,000). Now of course, if the quality of service isn't high, then no amount of cost savings is going to make up for it – but if you can combine high quality with reasonable cost, then you have something worth thinking about, and such is the case here.

Algodones is Mexico's northernmost town, and it caters primarily to Americans looking for heavily discounted medical and dental care as well as prescriptions and eyeglasses. It's said that within a four-block radius there are more pharmacies, doctors, dentists, and opticians than anywhere else in the world. Whether that's true or not we don't know, but it certainly is a happening little place, and it feels quite safe.

The oral surgeon/endodontist who performed Robin's root canal – Dr. Gaspar at Simply Dental – has 32 years of experience, and Robin felt the care she received was both professional and attentive. In fact it was one of the least painful procedures she has ever experienced. Her dentist spoke basic English, but his nephew who is also an oral surgeon spoke flawless English, and he was on hand to answer any questions she might have. The visit included a free exam and consult with free digital x-rays.

Like most dental offices in Algodones, the waiting area was small. In fact it was something of a shock to our American sensibilities when we first walked in the door and saw how simple and unpresuming it was. That said, it did have a Keurig coffee maker, bottled water, and wifi, and the dental equipment itself was state-of-the-art. Our sense was that no extra money was being spent on impressing us. Rather, as the name "Simply Dental" implied, the focus was on the quality of the dentistry itself.

Robin set up her appointment at no cost through the website Dental Departures (dentaldepartures.com). The website lists dentists from countries all around the world and offers helpful patient reviews and price lists for each. Robin chose her dentist after reading a string of glowing five-star reviews. The person she worked with at Dental Departures responded quickly to her emails and even arranged for her to speak directly to her dentist when she had some specific questions.

Rather than drive across the border (which is open from 6 am to 10 pm daily), we parked in a huge parking lot on the U.S. side for $5 per day and simply walked across, which is what most people do. (For mapping programs, use the border crossing address of 235 Andrade Road, Winterhaven, CA 92283.) We had plenty of company during our short walk. Literally hundreds of Americans, most of them seniors from the southwestern U.S., walk across this border point every day for low-cost medical and dental care.

The walk across the border into Mexico is a cinch: we just strolled right across. However, there is often a wait to get back through U.S. Customs. It can take an hour or more during the busiest times of day (usually 1-3 pm), but we went in the morning and came back before noon so there was only a short wait. We saw some people taking bicycle rickshaws in order to avoid the pedestrian line. Of course you should always be sure to have a valid U.S. passport with you.

Vision Tourism and Prescription Drugs

Robin needed some antibiotics related to her dentistry work, so we made a quick stop at The Purple Pharmacy in Algodones. Visitors have their pick of friendly and efficient pharmacies they can visit in the four-block area. Staff are eager to assist you, and chalk boards and handwritten signs prominently display prescription drug prices, making it easy to comparison shop.

It's legal to bring a 90-day supply of most antibiotics and other prescription drugs into the U.S., and Customs will check your purchases as you recross the border. It's helpful to know the generic name of the medication and the dosage you need before arriving in Algodones.

We haven't yet availed ourselves of the vision services offered in Algodones, but reports from other travelers suggest a typical eye exam runs about $10. Glasses start at $100 for two pairs of single-vision glasses with frames, and go up from there to $100-$150 per pair for more expensive progressive lenses. If vision coverage turns out to be minimal or nonexistent under the Affordable Care Act, then this becomes another compelling gap area in which early retirees might want to seek care abroad.

Judging from the number of visitors to this little town, we aren't the only ones who enjoy finding quality health care at affordable prices. Even our celebratory lunch of fish and shrimp tacos after Robin's dentist appointment was affordable and delicious. Which reminds us: don't forget the "tourism" part of medical tourism. Be sure to mix in a little fun along the way. Sure, there are practical aspects to your visit abroad, but remember that one of the main benefits of medical tourism is getting to do some sightseeing in a place that perhaps you've never been to before.

Chapter 17.
Extended Travel in Retirement

We retired early for one main reason: to travel more extensively and see the world. One of our greatest joys since retiring has been having no time limit on how long we can spend in another country seeing the sights and getting to know a different culture from the inside out. We prefer traveling slowly and on foot as much as possible, staying in a country for weeks or months at a time when we can, and that simply isn't feasible with a full-time job. We love to hike, so most of our trips include hiking or trekking in one form or another, and we usually choose natural scenery and small towns over big cities. Our personal website, wherewebe.com, gives you a good idea of the kind of travel we enjoy the most.

Over the past six years we've learned a fair amount about long-term travel and how it differs from short-term vacations. Extended travel requires a different mindset than your typical week-long getaway. In this final chapter we'd like to share a few suggestions about how you can travel more economically over longer periods of time should you wish to do so once you retire.

Picking Affordable Destinations

Choosing a low-cost destination is the single most important thing you can do to keep an extended trip affordable. Everything (other than airfare) becomes less expensive if the destination is inexpensive to start with. Lodging, dining out, groceries, transportation, guided tours, entry fees, activity fees, incidentals – all of it is much more reasonable in countries where your dollar goes further to start with.

If you pick your destination with care, you can easily live on less – sometimes significantly less – than you can in the U.S. In Ecuador, for example, we could buy apples and bananas for five cents each, an hour-long bus ride set us each back a dollar, and a double room with private bath ran us $15 to $20 per night. Lodgings rented by the month were cheaper still. With prices like these, you can see why retirees who come for a visit sometimes end up staying for good.

An even more dramatic example is India and Nepal, where we could live very well indeed on very little money. During a one-month hike of the Annapurna Circuit in Nepal, we stayed in teahouses for just $4 per night for a private room with bath. Admittedly the rooms were rustic, but $4 per night? Even when we stayed in Kathmandu, the capital city, a stylish and conveniently located midrange hotel with all the Western comforts of home only ran us $15 per night. Food in both India and Nepal was also inexpensive, delicious, and plentiful. We could essentially order whatever we wanted without regard to price.

That's not to say there aren't luxury accommodations and expensive restaurants in these and other low-cost countries, because of course there are. You can spend a lot of money even in an inexpensive country if you try hard enough, but it takes little effort on your part to live and eat well on low sums of money in destinations such as these.

Many times what you remember most about travel are the adventures and experiences you have along the way, and you can have more of them and at a lower price when you visit a low-cost destination. To cite just three examples, we were able to ride and bathe elephants in Nepal for $5, sail Superman-style on a zipline across a lush canyon in Ecuador for $12, and raft down the Yulong River in China on a bamboo raft for $5 while surrounded by spectacular views of limestone mountains. Consider what experiences similar to these might have cost in the U.S. – then double that again to determine what they might have cost in an expensive European country.

Often the only noteworthy expense involved in visiting a low-cost destination is the airfare to get there and back. That's one reason we like to stay for awhile once we reach a distant destination: it allows us to amortize the expense of the airfare over multiple months. (It also justifies all the effort to get there.) Once you've arrived, the living is actually cheaper than it is back home, so there's no particular rush: you might as well sit back, relax, and enjoy yourself for awhile.

Living abroad is frankly more fun when you don't feel crimped for money all the time. We would encourage you to look beyond the obvious Western European countries and broaden your focus to include places like Southeast Asia, Mexico, Central and South America, and Eastern Europe where your dollar will stretch further and buy you more.

Surviving Expensive Destinations

The most obvious strategy you can employ when visiting expensive foreign countries is simply to stay for shorter periods of time. Save your extended trips for countries where your dollar goes further. Plan shorter, more intensive sightseeing trips to countries where the dollar is working against you.

When we visit expensive destinations, we do things a little differently than we would otherwise in order to keep costs down. We eat more simply, sleep more simply, and choose our activities with more care. In some cases we research and pre-book lodgings ahead of time so we know what we're paying up front. We buy groceries and cook our own meals in, or else rely on simple takeout options. And we strategize ahead of time about how to keep our transportation costs down. For example, in Switzerland we purchased half-fare cards good for a month of train travel in-country, and in New Zealand we actually bought a used car then sold it back again four months later.

We try not to skimp on experiences, however, because after all, what's the point of visiting a place if you aren't really going to see it? A multi-day vaporetto pass is essential, for example, if you want to freely explore the canals of Venice. Similarly, a one-week cruise of the Galapagos Islands aboard a small yacht can be an integral part of the experience of seeing those islands well. Booking the trip last-minute and at half-price kept costs as reasonable as possible, but the final price tag was still unavoidably high (and worth every penny in our opinion).

You can't always cut corners and do a place justice. It would be a pity to miss out on dining al fresco in France or Italy, for instance, where food and wine are such an integral part of the pleasure of being there. Likewise it would be unfortunate to miss out on a thrilling adventure like bungee jumping or skydiving in a place like Queenstown, New Zealand ("adrenaline capital of the world") solely because of price. The memories from these experiences last a lifetime, and you only have to pay for them once.

So far we've managed to stay within our yearly budget of $40,000 even when our travel has taken us to expensive destinations like Switzerland and the Galapagos. Sometimes that has meant living more frugally the rest of the year, but we consider that a small price to pay for the privilege of getting to visit such unforgettable places. That said, the next time we visit Switzerland, we may not stay for quite so long!

Staying in Place vs. Moving Around

One important question you'll have to answer for yourself is this: do you prefer to base yourself in one place or move around a lot? Our own trips of late have typically involved moving every three or four days from one town to the next as we crisscross a country in order to see it well.

But near-constant movement has its price. Our expenses are higher than they would be otherwise because we're paying not only for transportation but also for lodging on a per-night basis. On the other hand, we get to see more of a country that way, and sometimes that outweighs the cost issues for us.

Without question, staying in one place for a month at a time or longer can be more cost-effective. We rented a room in Puerto Varas, Chile, for example, for less than $250 for the month – and Puerto Varas is a relatively expensive tourist town by Chilean standards.

To get a low monthly rate, it's best not to book ahead of time from the U.S. Instead, simply show up in the town or city of your choosing and stay at a hostel for a few days while scoping out longer-term rental possibilities. Many rentals only advertise locally with a sign in the window or a notice on a bulletin board. That's why we suggest you wait until you arrive in town before making long-term arrangements. That way you can see a rental with your own eyes before deciding if it's right for you.

Negotiating in person can also increase your bargaining power. Many owners will agree to a discount for stays of a month or longer, especially if you offer cash up front. If the room is obviously sitting empty and you're standing right there in front of them with cash in hand, they're more likely to accept a lower price.

Staying put offers a more relaxing way of traveling for an extended period of time. During our stay in Puerto Varas, for example, we went on excursions to surrounding towns and the nearby island of Chiloe. We took Spanish lessons at a tiny school across the street, and we traded informal English-for-Spanish lessons with local friends we made in town. Making friends is easier when you stay put for awhile, and taking language lessons or cooking classes or lessons in any sort of regional specialty can be a great way to get to know the locals and fellow travelers alike.

Discovering Your Own Approach to Travel

Knowing what makes you genuinely happy helps you determine your own approach to travel. If what you really love is staying in luxury hotels, there's no point in kidding yourself and pretending you like hostels. If five-star resorts with beachside service, spa treatments, and golf are more your speed, you'll simply have to factor in the higher costs of staying in such places. Perhaps you'll decide to travel for shorter periods of time but really pamper yourself when you do go.

On the other hand, if you're comfortable staying in simpler digs and like to walk around and explore on your own, then you can afford to stay much longer in the country of your choosing. Perhaps you'll immerse yourself in the local culture and begin picking up the language. Or perhaps you'll focus on seeing every sight you can while you're in-country, as we tend to do. Or maybe you'll just kick back and relax and soak it all in. After all, it's your trip: you can be as busy or as laid-back as you like.

There are so many variables to travel that it's hard to generalize, but if the question is, *can* you travel overseas affordably, the answer is definitely yes. Picking your destination with care is the number one thing you can do to lower your costs, and the second most important thing is to choose your lodgings with care, which is what we'll discuss next.

Staying in Hostels

When it comes to lodgings on a per-night basis, we think hostels offer the best value for your money. Hostels cater to all ages these days. Younger travelers tend to be their primary market, but as long as you're young at heart you'll fit right in. The accommodations are usually (but not always) on the basic side, so hostels are not for everyone, but if you dream of seeing the world on a budget while meeting friendly people and staying in the opposite of cookie-cutter accommodations, hostels just might be a right answer for you.

Shared kitchens make hostels a great option if you're trying to keep costs down, and free wifi access is almost a given these days. We always look for hostels offering double rooms (preferably with private bath) and not just dorm rooms. We prefer the privacy and security of having our own room.

You can pick up useful travel tips from fellow travelers at hostels, and each place you stay will be different from the next. To get an idea of just how memorable some hostel stays can be, check out the websites for Hopewell Backpackers in Marlborough Sound, New Zealand (hopewell.co.nz) and Palafito Hostel in Chiloe, Chile (palafitohostel.com).

Websites like hostelworld.com and bbh.co.nz (specific to New Zealand) assign a percentage ranking to each hostel based on the reviews of people who have stayed there, so you can quickly identify the best hostels in a particular area. Prices are listed for each type of room. These websites allow you to make an online booking a few days in advance, which can be a wise idea if you're traveling in high season.

Traveling Independently

The longer the trip you're planning, the more important it becomes to travel independently – that is, without a guide or as part of a tour group. Being on your own significantly reduces the cost of the trip, but perhaps equally importantly, it changes the whole tenor of the experience.

Travel becomes more of an adventure and less of a set piece when you make your own decisions about lodging, food, and activities. You get to determine your own pace and itinerary rather than turning those decisions over to another. You're also more likely to have genuine encounters with local residents if you travel independently. You'll strike up conversations on buses and trains, or when you're eating at small cafes not frequented by tour groups, or when you're staying at lodgings not specifically aimed at (and priced for) foreigners.

Independent travel can become addictive once you get used to it. It can be hard to go back to having someone tell you what to do, what to see, how long to see it for, and what time of day to go (often at midday, it seems, when crowds are at their worst).

Admittedly guided trips make sense under certain circumstances. If you're a female traveling alone, for example, or if logistical or language issues make planning a particular trip more intimidating than usual, then a guided excursion might be the right answer. But we would encourage you to wean yourself from only traveling in such a fashion, as it can dramatically increase your costs while diminishing your freedom to explore.

Researching Your Trip

Traveling independently means doing your own research beforehand or as you go along. It helps to have at least a rough idea ahead of time of where you want to go and what you'd like to see.

To get an initial sense of a country, we enjoy Frommer's free online travel guides, which cover just about every destination under the sun. Their introductory lists of favorite experiences and their reviews of key sights are highly readable. However, their lodging and dining information tends to be focused on the pricier end of the spectrum.

We usually end up buying a *Lonely Planet* guidebook for each country we visit, in part for the attention they give to economical lodging and dining options, but more importantly for their exceptional regional and city maps. We cut out only the pages we need and staple them together for a particular city or region so we can bring just those pages along with us on any particular day of exploring.

We've come to rely more and more on sites like Trip Advisor for ideas on the best things to do and the best places to stay in a particular location. The reviews of hundreds of individual travelers, taken as a whole and then ranked, seem to provide more consistently satisfying and up-to-date results for activities, lodging, and dining than any single guidebook can. Individual reviewers are also more apt to comment on the negative aspects of a particular option, giving you a more complete picture than you might get otherwise from a tersely worded guidebook description.

Managing Your Finances Overseas

An important practical consideration before your first extended trip is how to manage your finances while overseas. Fortunately this has become much easier now that electronic bill paying is so commonplace. We pay most of our bills automatically through our credit card, and the rest are paid through automatic deductions from our checking account. It's easy to set these up by visiting the website for each of your service providers and updating your account information to allow for automatic monthly payments. We recommend you do this a few months in advance of your trip so you can make sure everything is working properly before you leave.

Your bank's online bill pay service can also be a useful feature in case you have to make an unexpected payment from the other side of the world.

Using ATMs Overseas

When overseas we rely primarily on ATMs for cash. We pay a bank fee each time we withdraw money (typically $5), which can be annoying, but it's cheaper than most other options. We usually withdraw the maximum amount the ATM will allow in order to minimize these charges. In some countries the maximum amounts set by banks can be frustratingly low, so we end up searching around for ATMs with a higher limit that also happen to be compatible with the PLUS system our card utilizes.

Make sure your ATM withdrawal limits are set sufficiently high by your own bank. This is especially important if you are visiting a country where the local currency is stronger than the U.S. dollar. If you're married, it makes sense to carry a second card in your spouse's name so you can double-dip from the same account when needed.

ATMs typically provide you with local currency, so you don't have to worry about currency exchange, but you might need to visit a local bank now and again to obtain smaller bills.

Using Credit Cards Overseas

In first-world countries we often rely on our credit card instead of cash when making purchases. We pay a 1% fee for each international purchase, which isn't too bad. Check with your credit card company to see what rate you have to pay for international purchases. Some cards have rates as high as 3%, which is too high in our opinion if you're planning on staying overseas for an extended period of time. If your percentage is too high, consider applying for a credit card with no international purchase fee and using it specifically for travels abroad.

It's a good idea to carry a backup credit card from a completely different financial institution in case the first one gets lost, stolen, or invalidated. More than once our credit card has been canceled while we were traveling overseas due to a compromised batch of credit card numbers having been stolen from one store or another back in the States. Another card was immediately reissued and mailed to our home address in the U.S., but that did us little good since we were still abroad. Now we've learned our lesson and always carry a backup card.

Downsizing for Life on the Road

When you're planning for a mobile life on the road, you want to do all you can to downsize your electronics and other possessions so you can pack as lightly as possible. If you plan to travel with a laptop computer, be sure to get a lightweight and compact one. A pocketsize Canon PowerShot camera with a charger and extra battery gives us all we need for taking quality photos. We also bring iPod Shuffles for music and a tiny handheld microphone and ear buds for Skyping. We rely primarily on email and Skype to stay in touch with family and friends when traveling.

A small PacSafe mesh-lined bag lets us lock up passports and other sensitive documents while we're away from our room, and a simple locking cable helps keep our laptop safe.

A small daypack holds all our electronics and incidentals and fits inside our larger bag when we walk from point to point. When we get to the bus or taxi, we can pull out the daypack filled with the electronics, passports, and other things we really care about and keep it close at hand, while allowing our bigger bags filled with clothes to be stored worry-free in the vehicle's outer compartment or trunk.

We use Rick Steves convertible carry-on bags that convert into backpacks for nearly all of our trips, and we swear by them. If you can comfortably fit all your belongings into one of these bags, then you're doing quite well packing-wise. If the bag is bursting at the seams, then you're probably bringing too much and should try to lighten up a bit.

Every experienced traveler will tell you the same thing: less is more. You'll enjoy yourself more if you aren't burdened down like a pack animal. Try dressing in layers, and limit your bulky outer layers as much as possible. You can always buy an extra sweater on the road if needed.

Quality raingear that packs into its own pocket is always worth having. That plus a lightweight fleece jacket goes a long way towards keeping you warm in inclement weather.

Forwarding Physical Mail

As far as physical mail goes, we've found the maximum time permitted for holding mail at the local post office is thirty days. That usually isn't enough time for us, so instead we temporarily forward our mail to a relative's address. You can set this up online at usps.com, specifying the temporary address and the start and end dates. The maximum initial length of time for temporary forwarding is six months, but you can renew for another six months if needed. Note that you'll have to enter a credit card number for verification purposes when you use this online service, and there is a $1 charge to your card. Save the confirmation email sent to you so you can extend or cancel the forwarding order as needed.

Using Seasonal Disconnects

We use a seasonal disconnect service for both cable and internet to reduce costs when we're away for an extended period of time. For our service with Comcast, the disconnect has to be between 3 and 6 months in duration, and you still must pay $11 per service per month even though you aren't using it. At present you have to make a phone call to set up the seasonal disconnect; there is no online option.

Your service restarts automatically on the date you set, or else you can call if you get back sooner than expected to start it up again. There is no fee to disconnect or reconnect the service.

Becoming a Perpetual Traveler

If you plan to be a perpetual traveler or an RVer without a permanent home address, consider making a state with no income tax your official residence. You must call somewhere home, so you might as well pick a state that doesn't tax you for the privilege of not being there.

We tried this approach ourselves for a period of two years. After selling our home in Colorado, we headed off on an eight-month road trip through the U.S., traveling in a conversion van with a bed in the back. We also traveled overseas for extended periods of time to places like Argentina and Chile. During these two years we listed South Dakota as our home address. South Dakota has no state income tax, nor does it require yearly vehicle inspections or emissions tests.

My Dakota Address (mydakotaaddress.com) is a particularly useful service for perpetual travelers. They can help you register your vehicle and get you set up as a resident of South Dakota. You'll need to take an eye exam in person to obtain a South Dakota driver's license, but not much else is required.

My Dakota Address forwards your physical mail on a weekly or monthly basis for a reasonable fee, provides you with a physical address that doesn't appear as a P.O. box (useful when filling out forms), and generally makes your perpetual traveling life easier. If we ever decide to sell our condo and recommit to the nomadic lifestyle, we'll probably make South Dakota our home address once again and use this same service.

For those of our readers who have made it this far, we want to wish you every success during your own journey. Achieving early retirement is in many ways only the beginning: from there the doors open wide and the world is yours to explore. Here's hoping our paths may cross one day in some far-off corner of the world!

Appendix A.
Detailed Salary and Investment Information

Annual Salaries

Year	Age	Gross Salary			Total Net Salary
		Robert	Robin	Combined	
1990	27	$9,012	$14,440	$23,452	$18,712
1991	28	$10,104	$14,490	$24,594	$18,621
1992	29	$22,905	$15,100	$38,005	$30,611
1993	30	$27,169	$23,490	$50,659	$38,998
1994	31	$31,499	$24,429	$55,928	$41,799
1995	32	$44,273	$17,811	$62,084	$40,309
1996	33	$43,435	$18,250	$61,685	$40,534
1997	34	$38,754	$18,126	$56,880	$40,652
1998	35	$43,983	$15,113	$59,096	$39,221
1999	36	$56,891	$1,828	$58,719	$41,976
2000	37	$63,452	$38,840	$102,292	$67,253
2001	38	$75,594	$44,646	$120,240	$77,498
2002	39	$73,387	$50,480	$123,867	$81,866
2003	40	$74,415	$53,566	$127,981	$86,526
2004	41	$79,353	$54,506	$133,859	$89,796
2005	42	$90,000	$52,403	$142,403	$94,063
2006	43	$93,759	$49,754	$143,513	$94,835
AVG (15 yrs)		$57,258	$31,889	$89,147	$60,396

15 years from home purchase in Nov '91 to early retirement in Dec '06

Annual Amount Invested and Cumulative Nest Egg

Year	Age	Total Net Salary	Taxable	401k/IRA	Combined	% of Net Salary	Cumulative Nest Egg*
1992	29	$30,611	$0	$300	$300	1%	$415
1993	30	$38,998	$0	$833	$833	2%	$1,848
1994	31	$41,799	$2,500	$1,606	$4,106	10%	$6,578
1995	32	$40,309	$2,500	$5,812	$8,312	21%	$23,413
1996	33	$40,534	$5,000	$6,680	$11,680	29%	$45,122
1997	34	$40,652	$11,025	$3,280	$14,305	35%	$57,721
1998	35	$39,221	$8,650	$7,161	$15,811	40%	$72,042
1999	36	$41,976	$5,650	$10,464	$16,114	38%	$112,339
2000	37	$67,253	$19,150	$10,916	$30,066	45%	$128,276
2001	38	$77,498	$33,250	$10,698	$43,948	57%	$168,203
2002	39	$81,866	$26,850	$13,170	$40,020	49%	$184,314
2003	40	$86,526	$24,250	$13,608	$37,858	44%	$296,000
2004	41	$89,796	$19,250	$14,111	$33,361	37%	$396,529
2005	42	$94,063	$27,250	$17,103	$44,353	47%	$480,222
2006	43	$94,835	$31,750	$9,377	$41,127	43%	$626,219
15-yr AVG		**$60,396**	**$14,472**	**$8,341**	**$22,813**	**33.2%**	–

*Nest egg in chart does not include home equity of about $300,000 (as of 2006)

Net Assets in Retirement

Year	Age	Stocks	Bonds/Cash	Real Estate (Home then Condo)	Net Assets (As of 12/31 Each Year)
2006	43	$587,525	$38,694	$300,000	$926,219
2007	44	$627,356	$299,162	$0	$926,518
2008	45	$378,910	$304,082	$0	$682,992
2009	46	$485,743	$193,431	$100,000	$779,174
2010	47	$574,267	$206,030	$100,000	$880,297
2011	48	$534,865	$221,461	$100,000	$856,326
2012	49	$618,362	$208,269	$100,000	$926,631

← (Portfolio high of $975,000 Oct 2007)

Appendix B.
Creating Your Own Investment Spreadsheet

If you would prefer to create your own investment spreadsheet from scratch rather than downloading the template on our webpage (wherewebe.com), we provide detailed instructions here. These instructions may also be useful for those of you who downloaded the spreadsheet but aren't familiar with a program like Excel and need a bit more help.

When creating your own spreadsheet from scratch, be sure to use a spreadsheet program like Microsoft Excel that can automatically add columns of data, apply simple formulas to calculate annual rates of return, and add together results from one column to the next. That will allow you to tweak the spreadsheet to play with different investment scenarios. You can make changes and instantly see the results to the bottom line.

A sample investment spreadsheet is provided in Chapter 10. You may want to have a look at that first to get an overview of what the spreadsheet looks like in terms of column sizes and layout. We chose to use a landscaped 11" x 17" paper size to give ourselves plenty of room to work with, but the spreadsheet can also fit on a landscaped 8½" x 11" sheet of paper.

Now let's have a look at each column in the spreadsheet and see what's involved in reproducing it. For cells that contain formulas, we've used italics to identify the specific Excel formula that needs to be added to each cell in the column. None of the formulas are particularly complicated.

Taxable Columns

Column A – Year: Manually enter the years as necessary. To edit them, simply click on the cell, type in the correct information, and hit enter. You can delete rows at the bottom of the spreadsheet to create a 15-year plan. (Be sure to select the entire row by clicking on the row number to the left then hitting delete.) If you want a 25-year plan, you can copy and paste existing rows to add more years (again, be sure to select the entire rows).

Column B – Amount Invested: Manually enter the amount you plan to invest per year in your taxable account (i.e., any money you're setting aside for use before you turn age 59½). You can try out alternate savings scenarios by entering different numbers and seeing how the totals change.

Column C – Plus Prev. Year Total: This column automatically adds the "Total Taxable" (Column E) amount from last year to the "Amount Invested" (Column B) this year. *The formula in cell C6 for example (which shows $2,000 in the sample spreadsheet) is: =E5+B6.*

Column D – Annual % Return: This column automatically calculates the annual return generated from the amount in Column C. You can change the percentage by entering the cell (double-click on it) and changing the number – for example, from the default 0.09 (for 9%) to 0.08 (for 8%) or 0.1 (for 10%) or any other percentage you wish to experiment with. You can then copy and paste this cell to all other applicable cells below it. *The formula in cell D6 for example (which shows $180 in the sample spreadsheet) is: =C6*0.09.*

Column E – Total Taxable: This column automatically adds the amounts in Columns C and D to give your total taxable amount for the year. *The formula in cell E6 for example (which shows $2,180 in the sample spreadsheet) is: =C6+D6.*

Column F is a blank column for spacing.

401(k) Columns

Column G – Amount Invested: Manually enter the amount you plan to invest per year in your 401(k). You can try out various scenarios by entering different numbers and seeing the results.

Column H – Match: Automatically calculates a 401(k) match for you. The default is set to 50% of the amount in Column G. The percentage can be changed to bring it in line with the particulars of your 401(k) plan. Double-click on the first cell you would like to update and change the percentage – for example, from "0.5" (50%) to "1.0" (100%). You can then copy and paste this cell to all other applicable cells below it. *The formula in cell H6 for example (which shows $2,000 in the sample spreadsheet) is: =G6*0.5.*

Column I – Plus Prev. Year Total: Automatically adds the "Total 401(k)" (Column K) amount from last year to the "Amount Invested" (Column G) and "Match" (Column H) for this year. *The formula in cell I6 for example (which shows $6,000 in the sample spreadsheet) is: =K5+G6+H6.*

Column J – Annual % Return: Automatically calculates the annual return generated from the amount in Column I. (See Column D instructions for changing the percentage rate.) *The formula in cell J6 for example (which shows $540 in the sample spreadsheet) is: =I6*0.09.*

Column K – Total 401(k): Automatically adds the amounts in Columns I and J to give you your total 401(k) amount for the year. *The formula in cell K6 for example (which shows $6,540 in the sample spreadsheet) is: =I6+J6.*

Column L is a blank column for spacing.

Roth IRA Columns

Column M – Amount Invested: Manually enter the amount you plan to invest per year in your Roth IRA. As with the other shaded columns in the spreadsheet, you can try out different scenarios by entering different numbers and seeing the results.

Column N – Plus Prev. Year Total: Automatically adds the "Total Roth IRA" (Column P) amount from last year to the "Amount Invested" (Column M) for this year. *The formula in cell N6 for example (which shows $4,000 in the sample spreadsheet) is: =P5+M6.*

Column O – Annual % Return: Automatically calculates the annual return generated from the amount in Column N. (See Column D above for instructions on changing the percentage rate.) *The formula in cell O6 for example (which shows $360 in the sample spreadsheet) is: =N6*0.09.*

Column P – Total Roth IRA: Automatically adds the amounts in Columns N and O to give you your total Roth IRA amount for the year. *The formula in cell P6 for example (which shows $4,360 in the sample spreadsheet) is: =N6+O6.*

Column Q is a blank column for spacing.

Grand Total Column

Column R – Grand Total: Automatically adds the amounts in Columns E, K, and P (i.e., the totals for taxable, 401(k), and Roth IRA) to give you the grand total for the year. *The formula in cell R6 for example (which shows $13,080 in the sample spreadsheet) is: =E6+K6+P6.*

Made in the USA
San Bernardino, CA
13 July 2017